DEDALO AGENCY

PARIS

Travel guide

HOW TO PLAN
A TRIP TO PARIS
WITH BEST TIPS
FOR FIRST-TIMERS

Edited by: Domenico Russo and Francesco Umbria
Design e layout: Giorgia Ragona
Book series: Journey Joy

PARIS
Travel guide

Foreword

In the following pages of the book, you will find essential advice on what to see and do in Paris, and there will be specific insights to enjoy your trips to the fullest (even without spending exorbitant amounts).

The travel guide series of the Journey Joy collection was designed to be lean and straight to the point. The idea of keeping the guides short required significant work in synthesis, in order to guide the reader towards the essential destinations and activities within each country or city.

If you like the book, leaving a positive review can help us spread our work. We realize that leaving a review can be a tedious activity, so we want to give you a gift. Send an email to **bonus@dedaloagency.net**, attach the screenshot of your review, and you will get completely **FREE**, in your mailbox, **THE UNRELEASED EBOOK**: "The Art of Traveling: Essential Tips for Unforgettable Journeys".

Remember to check the Spam folder, as the email might end up there!

We thank you in advance and wish you to always travel and enjoy every adventure!

Index

FOREWORD   4
INTRODUCTION   11

CHAPTER 1: PARIS CENTRAL   17
  The Eiffel Tower   17
  The Louvre   18
  Notre Dame Cathedral   19
  Champs-Élysées   19
  Seine River Cruise   20
  Montmartre   20
  The Panthéon   21
  Luxembourg Gardens   21
  Opera Garnier   22
  Final Thoughts   23

CHAPTER 2: HISTORICAL PARIS   27
  Les Invalides   28
  The Conciergerie   28
  The Bastille   29
  Rodin Museum   30
  Paris Catacombs   30
  Cluny Museum   31
  Châtelet Area   32
  Place des Vosges   33
  Shoah Memorial   33
  Day Trip to Versailles   34
  Day Trip to Fontainebleau   35
  Final Thoughts   35

CHAPTER 3: ROMANTIC PARIS   41

Seine River Banks   41
Pont Alexandre III   42
Wall of "I Love Yous"   43
Parc des Buttes-Chaumont   43
Place Vendôme   44
Palais Royal   45
Île de la Cité and Île Saint-Louis   45
Sacre-Coeur Basilica   46
Sainte-Chapelle   47
Day Trip to Giverny   47
Final Thoughts   48

CHAPTER 4: MODERN PARIS   53

Centre Pompidou   53
La Villette Park   54
La Défense   55
Arab World Institute   55
Orsay Museum   56
Palais de Tokyo   57
Paris Philharmonic   57
Science and Industry Museum   58
Bercy Village   58
Fondation Louis Vuitton   59
Day Trip to Disneyland Paris   60
Final Thoughts   60

CHAPTER 5: ARTISTIC PARIS   65

Louvre Museum   65
Orangerie Museum   66
Picasso Museum   66
Montmartre Artists Square   67
Musée Marmottan Monet   68
Art Galleries in Le Marais   68
Street Art in Belleville   69
Musée de Montmartre   69
Musée national Gustave Moreau   70
Musée Jacquemart-André   70
Final Thoughts   71

CHAPTER 6: PARISIAN CUISINE — 75

- French Pastries — 75
- Cheese and Wine — 76
- Haute Cuisine — 76
- Street Food — 77
- Cafés and Bistros — 78
- Chocolate and Macarons — 79
- French Bread and Croissants — 79
- Cooking Classes — 80
- Food Markets — 80
- Final Thoughts — 81

CHAPTER 7: SHOPPING IN PARIS — 85

- Flea Markets — 85
- Fashion Boutiques — 86
- Bookshops — 87
- Galleries Lafayette — 87
- Le Marais Shops — 88
- Antique Shops — 88
- Day Trip to La Vallée Village — 89
- Final Thoughts — 90

CHAPTER 8: NIGHTLIFE IN PARIS — 95

- Cabarets and Shows — 95
- Jazz Clubs — 96
- Rooftop Bars — 97
- Nightclubs — 97
- Cinema and Film — 98
- Final Thoughts — 99

CHAPTER 9: OFF THE BEATEN PATH — 103

- Canal Saint-Martin — 103
- La Campagne à Paris — 104
- Les Arènes de Lutèce — 104
- Parc de Bercy — 105
- Musée de la Chasse et de la Nature — 105
- Little Tokyo — 106
- Chinatown — 107
- Belleville and Ménilmontant — 107
- La Petite Ceinture — 108

INDEX — 7

Day Trip to Vincennes Forest   108
Final Thoughts   109

CHAPTER 10: PARIS THROUGH THE SEASONS   115

Spring in Paris   115
Summer in Paris   116
Autumn in Paris   117
Winter in Paris   118
Dining Out   119
Seasonal Shopping   119
Cultural Activities   120
Outdoor Activities   121
Festivals and Traditions   122
Practical Tips   122
Final Thoughts   123

CHAPTER 11: HOW TO TRAVEL PARIS ON A BUDGET   129

Budget Accommodation   129
Eating on a Budget   130
Public Transport   131
Free Attractions   131
Budget Shopping   132
Cheap Flight and Train Tips   132
Discount Cards   133
Off-Season Travel   134
Final Thoughts   134

CHAPTER 12: 10 CULTURAL EXPERIENCES YOU MUST TRY IN PARIS 139

1 - French Cinema   139
2 - French Music   140
3 - French Theatre   141
4 - French Literature   141
5 - Wine Tasting   142
6 - Fashion Shows   143
7 - French Language   144
8 - French Sports   144
9 - French Festivals   145
10 - French Architecture   146

CHAPTER 13: PARISIAN WALKS   151

Tips for Walking in Paris   151
1 - Montmartre Walk   153
2 - Le Marais Stroll   154
3 - Latin Quarter Wander   155
4 - St-Germain-des-Prés Promenade   156
5 - Canal St-Martin Amble   157
6 - Belleville Ramble   158
7 - Île de la Cité and Île Saint-Louis Saunter   159
8 - Champs-Élysées and Tuileries Trek   160
Final Thoughts   161

CHAPTER 14: RECOMMENDED ITINERARY IN PARIS   167

3-Day Itinerary   168
5-Day Itinerary   171
Final Thoughts   172

CONCLUSION   174
FINAL NOTES   178

INDEX   9

Introduction

Hello dear reader, welcome to this journey to discover Paris, the city of love, art, fashion, and gastronomy. Yes, Paris is all of this and much more. No matter how many times you've visited, this city always has something new to offer. And if it's your first time, prepare to fall head over heels in love.

This book was created with the idea of being your ideal travel companion, offering you not only a detailed guide to the most iconic and beloved places in Paris but also suggestions on less known but equally fascinating places. We want to share with you not only the postcard Paris but also the Paris of Parisians, the secret Paris that only locals really know.

Throughout this book, we will accompany you through the most fascinating neighborhoods of Paris, sharing with you stories and anecdotes that will enrich your travel experience. From the magic of the Eiffel Tower to the bohemian charm of Montmartre, from the hidden masterpieces of the Louvre to the architectural treasures of Le Marais, this book will guide you step by step through all that Paris has to offer.

Each chapter of this book is dedicated to a specific aspect of the city. From its history to its monuments, from its cuisine to its nightlife. We have also included chapters dedicated to tips for traveling on a limited budget and suggestions for unmissable cultural experiences.

But that's not all. We have also included a recommended itinerary of 3 and 5 days, to help you organize your trip so you can see the best of Paris, regardless of the time you have available. This itinerary includes both the most iconic places and the lesser-known ones, for a truly complete travel experience.

We want you to experience Paris like a Parisian, and that you can take home unforgettable memories. So, grab a baguette, a glass of red wine, and let's start this journey together. Paris awaits you, and we are sure it will be an unforgettable adventure.

With this spirit, we want you to know that this book is not just a simple tourist guide. It is an invitation to live Paris in all its glory, discovering its most secret corners and its most fascinating stories. It is an invitation to get lost in its streets, to sip coffee in a small bistro, to have a picnic in one of its beautiful parks.

In this book, we offer you a complete view of Paris, which goes well beyond the standard list of tourist places to visit. Of course, we will talk about the Eiffel Tower, the Louvre, and Notre-Dame. But we will also talk about local markets, antique shops, literary cafes, and lesser-known neighborhoods.

We will talk about Parisian cuisine, from the most traditional dishes to the most innovative restaurants. We will give you advice on where to eat, what to order, and how to best enjoy the Parisian gastronomic experience.

We will talk about the history of Paris, from its Roman origins to its most recent transformations. We will tell you the stories of the people who contributed to making Paris the city it is today, from artists to revolutionaries, from writers to politicians.

And, of course, we will talk about the romantic side of Paris, the city of love par excellence. We will give you tips for a romantic getaway, from the most iconic places to the most intimate and hidden ones.

In short, this book is a tribute to Paris, a city that has fascinated and inspired millions of people from all over the world. We hope it will become your trusted companion on your journey to discover the city of light.

Ready? Let's start our journey together. Paris awaits us!

CHAPTER 1:
Paris Central

Paris, the capital of France, is often referred to as "The City of Light" due to its pivotal role in the Age of Enlightenment, but also literally because it was one of the first cities in the world to have street lighting. The city is known worldwide for its art, gastronomy, and culture. Geographically split into 20 districts, twisted in a snail shape starting from the center of the city, Paris has a lot to offer. From iconic landmarks like the Eiffel Tower and the Louvre to lesser-known gems like the Luxembourg Gardens and the Panthéon, this chapter will guide you through the heart of Paris.

Remember, while the landmarks are breathtaking, take some time to also enjoy the simple pleasures - a stroll along the Seine, a cup of coffee in a sidewalk cafe, or a leisurely afternoon in a city park. Embrace the Parisian way of life, and you'll leave with a deeper appreciation of the city.

The Eiffel Tower

The Eiffel Tower, or "La Tour Eiffel" in French, is one of the most recognizable structures in the world and a must-see on any trip to Paris. Designed by Gustave Eiffel for the 1889 Exposition Universelle (World Fair), it held the title of the world's tallest man-made structure until 1930. Today, it stands as a symbol of Paris and a testament to human ingenuity and creativity.

Visitors can take the elevator or, if you're feeling energetic, climb the stairs to the second level. For an unforgettable experience, consider booking a dinner reservation at the 58 Tour Eiffel restaurant, which offers breathtaking views of the city. And don't forget to see the Eiffel Tower at night - it's illuminated with thousands of twinkling lights, and there's a light show every evening.

Lastly, while the Eiffel Tower is a sight to behold, be prepared for long lines and crowds, especially during peak tourist seasons. Consider booking your tickets online in advance to skip the lines and save time.

The Louvre

The Louvre Museum, or "Musée du Louvre" in French, is the world's largest and most visited museum. It is home to over 380,000 objects, including the famous Mona Lisa and The Venus de Milo. Housed in the Palais du Louvre, a former royal palace, the museum is a masterpiece in itself, with its glass pyramid entrance becoming an iconic symbol of Paris.

Plan your visit carefully, as it's virtually impossible to see everything in one day. Consider taking a guided tour or focusing on a specific collection that interests you the most. Also, remember to take breaks and enjoy the beautiful surroundings - the Tuileries Garden is right next door and is a perfect spot for a leisurely stroll or a picnic.

Lastly, the Louvre can get very crowded, especially during peak tourist seasons. Consider visiting on a Wednesday or Friday evening when the museum is open until 9:45 pm and tends to be less crowded. And, of course, don't forget to book your tickets online in advance to avoid long lines at the entrance.

Notre Dame Cathedral

The Notre Dame Cathedral, or "Cathédrale Notre-Dame de Paris" in French, is one of the most famous cathedrals in the world and a masterpiece of Gothic architecture. Located on the Île de la Cité, a small island in the center of Paris, the cathedral's construction began in 1163 and took almost 200 years to complete. Its intricate facade, stunning rose windows, and impressive flying buttresses make it a must-visit site in Paris.

Visitors can explore the interior of the cathedral, climb to the top for panoramic views of the city, or attend a mass. Keep in mind, though, that Notre Dame is still an active place of worship, so please be respectful of any services taking place.

Lastly, as you may know, the cathedral suffered significant damage in a fire in 2019. Restoration work is ongoing, and while parts of the cathedral may be closed to the public, it's still worth a visit to see this iconic landmark and the restoration efforts.

Champs-Élysées

The Avenue des Champs-Élysées, commonly known simply as the Champs-Élysées, is one of the most famous avenues in the world. Stretching for almost 2 kilometers (1.2 miles) between the Place de la Concorde and the Arc de Triomphe, it is lined with theaters, cafes, and luxury shops. The avenue is also the finish line for the Tour de France cycling race.

Strolling down the Champs-Élysées is a quintessential Parisian experience. Stop for a coffee or a meal at one of the many cafes, do some window shopping, or simply enjoy the bustling atmosphere. At the western end of the avenue, you'll find the Arc de Triomphe, another iconic Parisian landmark.

Lastly, keep in mind that the Champs-Élysées can be very crowded, especially on weekends and during peak tourist seasons. Keep an eye on your belongings and be aware of your surroundings.

Seine River Cruise

The Seine River, which winds its way through the heart of Paris, is one of the city's most iconic features. A cruise on the Seine offers a unique perspective of Paris and allows you to see many of the city's most famous landmarks from the water, including the Eiffel Tower, Notre Dame Cathedral, and the Louvre.

There are many different cruise options available, from simple sightseeing tours to dinner cruises with gourmet meals. Most cruises last about an hour and offer commentary in multiple languages. If you're looking for a romantic experience, consider taking an evening cruise when the city's landmarks are beautifully illuminated.

Lastly, remember that the Seine is a busy river with a lot of boat traffic. Book your cruise in advance, especially during peak tourist seasons, and consider taking a cruise at off-peak times for a more relaxed experience.

Montmartre

Montmartre is a historic and artistic neighborhood located on a hill in the 18th arrondissement of Paris. It's known for its bohemian atmosphere, narrow streets, and artistic heritage. Many famous artists, including Picasso, Van Gogh, and Dali, lived and worked here. The area is dominated by the Sacré-Cœur Basilica, a white-domed church that offers stunning views of Paris.

Exploring Montmartre can feel like stepping back in time. Visit the Place du Tertre, where artists display their work and offer portraits, or the former studios of famous artists, now turned into museums. And don't forget to stop at a traditional café for a coffee or a glass of wine.

Lastly, Montmartre can be quite crowded, especially on weekends and during peak tourist seasons. It's also quite hilly, so wear comfortable shoes and take your time exploring. If you want to avoid the crowds, consider visiting early in the morning or late in the afternoon.

The Panthéon

The Panthéon is a neoclassical mausoleum located in the Latin Quarter of Paris. It contains the remains of many distinguished French citizens, including Voltaire, Rousseau, and Marie Curie. The building's facade is modeled after the Pantheon in Rome, and its interior is adorned with beautiful frescoes and sculptures. Visitors can explore the crypt, where many famous French figures are interred, or climb to the colonnade for panoramic views of Paris. The Panthéon also has a Foucault pendulum, which demonstrates the rotation of the Earth.

Lastly, the Panthéon is an active place of commemoration, so please be respectful when visiting. Also, remember to check the opening hours and any special events or closures before you go.

Luxembourg Gardens

The Luxembourg Gardens, or "Jardin du Luxembourg" in French, are located in the 6th arrondissement of Paris. They were created in 1612 by Marie de' Medici, the widow of King

Henry IV of France. The gardens are beautifully landscaped with tree-lined promenades, fountains, and statues. There is also a large pond, where children can rent small boats.

Visitors can enjoy a leisurely stroll, have a picnic, or simply relax on one of the many chairs scattered throughout the gardens. The gardens are also home to the French Senate, housed in the Luxembourg Palace, and the Musée du Luxembourg, which hosts temporary art exhibitions.

Lastly, the Luxembourg Gardens are a popular spot for both locals and tourists, so they can get quite busy, especially on sunny days. If you're looking for a quieter experience, consider visiting early in the morning or during the week. And don't forget to check the opening hours, as they vary with the seasons.

Opera Garnier

The Palais Garnier, commonly known as the Opera Garnier, is one of the most famous opera houses in the world. It was built from 1861 to 1875 for the Paris Opera and is named after its architect, Charles Garnier. The building is a masterpiece of Beaux-Arts architecture and is adorned with marble grand staircases, chandeliers, and Marc Chagall-painted ceiling.

Visitors can take a guided tour of the opera house or attend a performance. The Opera Garnier hosts ballets, operas, and other performances throughout the year. It's advisable to book tickets in advance, as performances often sell out.

Lastly, the Opera Garnier is located in a busy part of Paris, so be mindful of your belongings. Also, remember to check the dress code if you are attending a performance, as it can be quite formal.

Final Thoughts

Paris, the City of Light, is a place where history, culture, and beauty intersect at every corner. While this chapter covers some of the most iconic landmarks and experiences, Paris has so much more to offer. From its quaint cobblestone streets and hidden courtyards to its lesser-known museums and local neighborhood markets, there is always something new to discover in Paris.

Additionally, Paris is a city that invites you to immerse yourself in its culture. Consider taking a cooking class to learn how to make classic French dishes, attend a language course to brush up on your French, or simply spend an afternoon people-watching at a sidewalk café. Paris is a city that encourages you to slow down, appreciate the finer things in life, and truly savor each moment.

In conclusion, a trip to Paris offers the opportunity to experience world-class art and architecture, indulge in exquisite cuisine, and immerse yourself in a culture that has inspired artists, writers, and thinkers for centuries. Whether it's your first visit or your tenth, Paris is always a good idea. Bon voyage!

CHAPTER 2:
Historical Paris

· ·

Paris, the capital city of France, is a treasure trove of history, a narrative that stretches back thousands of years. This chapter invites you on a journey through time, as we explore the landmarks that tell the tale of this captivating city. From its beginnings as a Roman settlement to its transformation during the French Revolution and its role in two World Wars, Paris has been the backdrop to many of history's most significant events. As you wander through its streets, you'll encounter echoes of the past around every corner; in the grandeur of its palaces, the dark dungeons of its prisons, and the elegant squares that have witnessed both celebration and revolution. With each step, you'll be walking in the footsteps of historical figures who shaped not only France but the world. This chapter will guide you through some of the most important historical sites in Paris, offering insights into the city's past and its enduring legacy.

You'll discover the stories behind the iconic monuments, the battles fought for freedom, and the artistic movements that changed the course of art history. And as you delve deeper into Paris's past, you'll uncover a city that is as intriguing as it is beautiful, a city that has inspired countless novels, paintings, and revolutions. Whether you're a history enthusiast, an art lover, or simply curious about the world, this chapter will provide a fresh perspective on the City of Light and its multifaceted history.

Les Invalides

The Hôtel National des Invalides, commonly known as Les Invalides, is a complex of buildings in the 7th arrondissement of Paris, containing museums and monuments, all relating to the military history of France. The most notable tomb at Les Invalides is that of Napoleon Bonaparte. This grand edifice is not only an important military monument but also a symbol of national pride.

Visiting Les Invalides offers a glimpse into the military history of France, from the medieval period to World War II. The Musée de l'Armée, housed within the complex, is home to an extensive collection of arms, armor, and military artifacts. Don't forget to visit the Dome Church, a masterpiece of French Baroque architecture, where Napoleon's tomb lies.

Les Invalides is vast, so be prepared to spend several hours if you want to see everything. It's also a good idea to purchase your ticket online to avoid the queues. And while you're in the area, consider taking a stroll along the Seine River or visiting the nearby Rodin Museum.

The Conciergerie

The Conciergerie is a historic building on the Île de la Cité in central Paris. It was originally a royal palace and later served as a prison during the French Revolution. Today, it is part of the larger Palais de Justice complex and is open to the public as a museum.

Visiting the Conciergerie provides a fascinating insight into the French Revolution, one of the most tumultuous periods in French history. The building itself is an architectural gem, with its medieval Hall of Soldiers, the Gothic Chapel, and the cells where prisoners, including Marie Antoinette, were held before their execution.

To make the most of your visit, consider joining a guided tour or renting an audio guide. This will provide you with a deeper understanding of the history and significance of the site. Also, if you plan to visit other nearby attractions such as the Sainte-Chapelle or the Notre Dame Cathedral, consider purchasing a combined ticket to save on entrance fees.

The Bastille

The Bastille was originally a fortress and later a state prison in Paris. It played a significant role in the internal conflicts of France and, most famously, was stormed by a crowd during the French Revolution in the 14th of July 1789. Today, the Place de la Bastille is a square where the prison stood until its destruction.

While the prison itself is long gone, the Place de la Bastille is still a symbol of the fight for liberty and the French Republic. The July Column stands in the center of the square, commemorating the revolution of 1830. The Opera Bastille, a modern opera house, is also located here.

Place de la Bastille is a bustling area with many cafes and restaurants. It's a great place to stop for a coffee and soak in the atmosphere. Also, check out the nearby Marché Bastille, a lively outdoor market held on Thursdays and Sundays.

Rodin Museum

The Rodin Museum, located in the 7th arrondissement of Paris, is dedicated to the works of the famous French sculptor Auguste Rodin. Housed in the beautiful Hôtel Biron, where Rodin himself once lived and worked, the museum boasts an extensive collection of over 6,000 sculptures, including some of his most famous works such as "The Thinker," "The Kiss," and "The Gates of Hell."

As you wander through the elegant rooms of the museum and the surrounding gardens, you'll get a sense of the artist's creative process and the evolution of his style. From his early works, influenced by traditional academic training, to his later pieces that broke with convention and paved the way for modern sculpture, Rodin's oeuvre is a testament to his genius and his enduring impact on the art world.

And while the sculptures are undoubtedly the main attraction, the museum also holds a collection of 7,000 drawings and prints, as well as photographs, letters, and personal objects that provide a glimpse into the artist's life and mind. Lastly, don't forget to stroll through the sculpture garden, a peaceful oasis in the heart of the city that features over 20 of Rodin's bronze sculptures set amidst beautifully landscaped grounds.

Paris Catacombs

The Paris Catacombs, located in the 14th arrondissement, are a network of underground tunnels that hold the remains of over six million people. Created in the 18th century to address the city's overflowing cemeteries, the catacombs have since become one of Paris's most unique and eerie attractions.

As you descend into the dark, cool tunnels, you'll be greeted by walls lined with neatly arranged skulls and bones, a stark reminder of the city's past and the transient nature of life. The catacombs are not just a final resting place, but also a fascinating historical site. The tunnels, which stretch for over 200 miles beneath the city, have a long and storied history. They have served as a hideout for French Resistance fighters during World War II, a canvas for street artists, and even a clandestine venue for secret parties. As you explore this labyrinthine network, you'll encounter inscriptions, sculptures, and other artifacts that reveal the many layers of history embedded within the walls. Remember to bring a light jacket as it can get quite chilly underground, and note that the catacombs are not recommended for those with claustrophobia or mobility issues.

Cluny Museum

The Cluny Museum, officially known as the Musée de Cluny - Musée national du Moyen Âge, is located in the 5th arrondissement and is home to one of the world's finest collections of medieval art and artifacts. Housed in two remarkable buildings, a 15th-century mansion and the ruins of a 3rd-century Roman bath, the museum offers a journey back in time to the Middle Ages.

As you wander through the atmospheric rooms, you'll encounter an array of treasures, from intricate tapestries and illuminated manuscripts to delicate ivories and stained glass. One of the museum's highlights is the famous "Lady and the Unicorn" tapestry series, a masterpiece of medieval art that is shrouded in mystery and allegory. The museum's collection is not just limited to art; it also includes everyday objects, religious relics, and archaeological finds that provide a glimpse into the daily life and beliefs of people living in the medieval period.

And while the objects on display are fascinating, the buildings themselves are also a highlight. The architecture, with its gothic arches, medieval stonework, and Roman ruins, provides a fitting backdrop for the collection and adds to the sense of stepping back in time. After your visit, take a leisurely stroll in the museum's peaceful garden, a hidden gem in the heart of the bustling Latin Quarter.

Châtelet Area

The Châtelet area, located in the 1st arrondissement of Paris, is a vibrant and bustling part of the city, steeped in history and culture. It's home to the Théâtre du Châtelet, a renowned theater that has hosted countless performances since its opening in 1862. The area is also known for its beautiful squares and open spaces, including the Place du Châtelet, a major public square that features the Fontaine du Palmier, a monumental fountain built to commemorate Napoleon's victories.

Besides its cultural landmarks, the Châtelet area is also a shopping and dining hotspot, with numerous boutiques, restaurants, and cafes lining its streets. Whether you're in the mood for high-end fashion, delicious French cuisine, or a leisurely stroll along the Seine, this area has something to offer. Don't miss a walk across the Pont au Change, a historic bridge that offers stunning views of the Seine and the surrounding architecture.

Since this area can get quite crowded, especially during peak tourist seasons, it's advisable to plan your visit during the early morning or late afternoon. Also, remember to keep an eye on your belongings as pickpocketing can be an issue in busy areas.

Place des Vosges

The Place des Vosges, located in the Marais district, is the oldest planned square in Paris and one of the most beautiful in the city. Built by Henri IV from 1605 to 1612, it is a perfect square, lined with symmetrical houses with red brick facades, steep pitched roofs, and large arcades on the ground floor. In the center of the square is a lovely garden, a perfect spot for a picnic or a leisurely afternoon.

Visiting the Place des Vosges is like stepping back in time. The uniformity and harmony of the architecture, the sense of history that permeates the air, and the relaxed atmosphere make it a must-visit spot in Paris. While there, don't forget to visit the Maison de Victor Hugo, the former home of the famous writer, which is now a museum dedicated to his life and works.

The Marais district surrounding the Place des Vosges is also worth exploring. Filled with narrow streets, boutiques, art galleries, and cafes, it's a lively and fashionable area with a rich history. Keep in mind that the Marais can get quite busy, especially on weekends, so plan your visit accordingly.

Shoah Memorial

The Shoah Memorial, located in the Marais district, is a museum and memorial dedicated to the Holocaust and the six million Jews who perished during World War II. Opened in 2005, the memorial includes a wall of names, listing the 76,000 Jews deported from France, of whom only 2,500 returned. It also features a multimedia library, a bookshop, and temporary exhibitions.

A visit to the Shoah Memorial is a powerful and sobering experience. The memorial does an excellent job of documenting the

Holocaust through photographs, documents, and personal tes-timonies. It serves as a reminder of the atrocities committed during this dark period in history and the importance of never forgetting them.

The Shoah Memorial is open every day except Saturdays and Jewish holidays. Admission is free, but donations are encour-aged. Keep in mind that the memorial may not be suitable for young children due to the graphic nature of some of the exhibits.

Day Trip to Versailles

The Palace of Versailles, located about 20 km southwest of Paris, is one of the most famous palaces in the world. It was originally a hunting lodge for King Louis XIII, but was transformed and expanded by his son, Louis XIV, into a magnificent palace. The palace and its gardens are a UNESCO World Heritage Site and a symbol of the absolute monarchy of the Ancien Régime.

Visiting Versailles is like stepping back into the grandeur of 17th and 18th century France. From the opulent Hall of Mirrors to the intricately landscaped gardens, there is much to see and do. Don't miss the Grand Trianon, a smaller palace on the grounds, and Marie Antoinette's estate, which includes the Petit Trianon and a recreated Norman village.

Lastly, Versailles can get extremely crowded, especially during peak tourist season. It's advisable to purchase tickets online in advance to avoid long lines. Also, consider visiting early in the morning or late in the afternoon for a more pleasant experience. And don't forget to wear comfortable shoes, as the palace and gardens are vast.

Day Trip to Fontainebleau

Fontainebleau, located about 55 kilometers southeast of Paris, is home to the magnificent Château de Fontainebleau, one of the largest and most beautiful royal châteaux in France. With over 1500 rooms set amidst 130 acres of parkland and gardens, Fontainebleau has been a residence of French monarchs from Louis VII to Napoleon III.

A visit to Fontainebleau is like a journey through the history of France. Each room in the château reflects the tastes and ambitions of the monarch who inhabited it. Don't miss the Renaissance rooms, the Gallery of Francis I, and the sumptuous apartments of Napoleon Bonaparte. The vast park and gardens, which include a large pond, ancient oaks, and meticulously maintained flowerbeds, are perfect for a leisurely stroll.

Getting to Fontainebleau from Paris is easy. Trains from Gare de Lyon in Paris to Fontainebleau-Avon take about 40 minutes, and from the Fontainebleau-Avon station, it's a short bus ride or a 20-minute walk to the château. It's advisable to arrive early to avoid the crowds and leave plenty of time to explore the château and its grounds.

Final Thoughts

As we conclude our journey through the historical side of Paris, it's hard not to be moved by the city's rich tapestry of history, art, and culture. From the solemnity of the Shoah Memorial to the opulence of Fontainebleau and the modernity of La Défense, Paris offers a fascinating glimpse into the past, present, and future.

But remember, while the landmarks and monuments are a must-see, the true heart of Paris lies in its neighborhoods, its cafes, and its people. Take the time to wander off the beaten path, sit in a local café, and watch the world go by. Paris is a city to be savored, not just seen.

Bon voyage, and may your journey through Paris be as enchanting and inspiring as the city itself.

CHAPTER 3:
Romantic Paris

Paris, often referred to as the 'City of Love', has long been a magnet for lovers and romantics from all around the world. From its beautiful Seine riverbanks and iconic bridges to its charming parks and squares, the city provides a perfect backdrop for romantic escapades.

In this chapter, we will guide you through some of the most romantic spots in Paris, locations that will make your heart flutter and possibly make you fall even deeper in love with this magnificent city.

Whether you are visiting with your significant other or simply wish to soak up the romantic atmosphere, these sites are sure to leave a lasting impression. Let's embark on a journey through the romantic side of Paris, one that will hopefully leave you with memories to cherish for a lifetime.

Seine River Banks

The Seine River, winding its way through the heart of Paris, is undoubtedly one of the most romantic spots in the city. The riverbanks, or 'quais' in French, offer a picturesque setting for a leisurely stroll, a sunset cruise, or a picnic. From the Eiffel Tower to Notre-Dame Cathedral, many of the city's iconic landmarks can be seen from the Seine.

Walking along the Seine River banks, you'll find numerous spots to sit and enjoy the view, street performers entertaining passersby, and bookstalls selling vintage books and postcards. And as the sun sets, the city lights up, creating a magical atmosphere that is perfect for an evening stroll.

If you're planning a visit to the Seine riverbanks, consider taking a cruise on one of the many boats that operate along the river. It's a great way to see the city from a different perspective and can be especially romantic at sunset or in the evening when the city is illuminated.

Pont Alexandre III

The Pont Alexandre III is one of the most beautiful bridges in Paris, spanning the Seine River and connecting the Invalides on the left bank to the Grand Palais and Petit Palais on the right bank. It was named after Tsar Alexander III, who had concluded the Franco-Russian Alliance in 1892, and its construction was a symbol of the friendship between France and Russia.

The bridge itself is a work of art, featuring ornate lampposts, cherubs, nymphs, and winged horses at either end. It offers stunning views of the Seine River, the Eiffel Tower, and the Invalides, making it a popular spot for both tourists and locals alike.

A walk across the Pont Alexandre III is a must for any visitor to Paris, and it's especially romantic in the evening when the bridge is illuminated. Consider bringing a camera to capture the moment, as the views from the bridge are some of the most photogenic in the city. And after your walk, why not enjoy a drink or a meal at one of the many cafés and restaurants located on either side of the river?

Wall of "I Love Yous"

The "Wall of I Love Yous" or "Le Mur des Je t'aime" in French, is located in the romantic neighborhood of Montmartre. It is a unique monument dedicated to love and affection. The wall features the words "I love you" written in over 250 languages and dialects, making it a symbol of universal love and a popular spot for both locals and tourists alike.

Visitors often come here to take photographs, to find the "I love you" in their own language, or simply to soak in the romantic atmosphere. The wall was created by artists Frédéric Baron and Claire Kito, who collected "I love you" in various languages from people all over the world. The result is a beautiful mosaic of love messages, which makes it a perfect spot for couples to visit.

If you plan on visiting the Wall of "I Love Yous," consider combining it with a stroll around Montmartre, one of the most romantic and artistic neighborhoods in Paris. After visiting the wall, you can explore the narrow streets, visit the artists' square, or enjoy a coffee in one of the many charming cafés in the area.

Parc des Buttes-Chaumont

The Parc des Buttes-Chaumont is one of the most beautiful parks in Paris and a perfect spot for a romantic walk or picnic. Located in the 19th arrondissement, this park offers stunning views of the city, beautiful waterfalls, and a picturesque lake. The park is also home to several species of birds, making it a great spot for bird-watching.

One of the highlights of the park is the Temple de la Sibylle, a miniature version of the ancient Roman Temple of Vesta in

Tivoli, Italy. Perched on a cliff above the lake, the temple is a popular spot for proposals and offers breathtaking views of the city.

If you plan on visiting the Parc des Buttes-Chaumont, consider bringing a picnic and spending a few hours relaxing in this beautiful oasis in the city. The park is also a great spot for jogging or a leisurely walk, and there are several playgrounds for children, making it a perfect destination for the whole family.

Place Vendôme

Place Vendôme is one of the most elegant squares in Paris, located in the 1st arrondissement. It is surrounded by luxurious hotels, high-end boutiques, and exquisite jewelry stores, making it a symbol of French luxury and refinement. At the center of the square stands the Vendôme Column, a monument inspired by Trajan's Column in Rome, and topped with a statue of Napoleon.

While Place Vendôme may not be a traditional romantic spot, its elegance and charm make it a popular destination for couples. Many come here to shop for jewelry or to stay in one of the luxurious hotels surrounding the square. It is also a popular spot for fashion photoshoots and a must-visit for those interested in luxury and fashion.

If you plan on visiting Place Vendôme, consider taking a walk around the square and admiring the beautiful architecture. Then, if your budget allows, treat yourself to a piece of jewelry from one of the famous boutiques or enjoy a meal in one of the nearby high-end restaurants. It's a perfect spot to experience the luxury and elegance of Paris.

Palais Royal

The Palais Royal, located in the 1st arrondissement, is a historic palace with beautiful gardens that offer a peaceful escape from the bustling city. The palace was originally built for Cardinal Richelieu in the 17th century and has since been home to various members of the French royalty.

While the palace itself is not open to the public, the gardens are a popular spot for both locals and tourists. The perfectly manicured lawns, elegant statues, and beautiful fountains make it a perfect spot for a leisurely stroll or a romantic picnic.

One of the highlights of the Palais Royal is the Cour d'Honneur, which features Daniel Buren's modern art installation, "Les Deux Plateaux" or "The Two Plateaus." This installation consists of black and white striped columns of varying heights, which have become an iconic symbol of the palace.

If you plan on visiting the Palais Royal, consider spending some time in the gardens, and don't forget to take a few photos in the Cour d'Honneur. Then, you can explore the surrounding area, which is home to several art galleries, antique shops, and cafés.

Île de la Cité and Île Saint-Louis

The Île de la Cité and Île Saint-Louis are two islands in the Seine River in the heart of Paris. These islands are home to some of the city's most iconic landmarks, including Notre-Dame Cathedral and the Sainte-Chapelle.

Île de la Cité is the larger of the two islands and is often referred to as the heart of Paris. It is home to several important historical sites, including the Palais de Justice and the Hôtel-Dieu, the oldest hospital in the city.

Île Saint-Louis, on the other hand, is smaller and more residential. It is home to beautiful 17th-century architecture, charming streets, and several art galleries and boutiques. It is also a great spot for a leisurely stroll along the Seine River.

If you plan on visiting the Île de la Cité and Île Saint-Louis, consider taking a walk along the riverbanks and exploring the charming streets. Then, you can visit Notre-Dame Cathedral and the Sainte-Chapelle, or simply relax in one of the many cafés on the islands.

Sacre-Coeur Basilica

Perched atop the highest point in Paris, Montmartre, the Sacre-Coeur Basilica is one of the most iconic landmarks in the city. The basilica is dedicated to the Sacred Heart of Jesus and offers stunning views of Paris from its steps.

The interior of the basilica is adorned with beautiful mosaics, and the atmosphere inside is serene and contemplative. It is a perfect spot for some quiet reflection or to light a candle for a loved one.

The area surrounding the basilica is also worth exploring. Montmartre has a bohemian atmosphere, with narrow, winding streets, art studios, and small cafés. It was once home to many famous artists, including Picasso and Van Gogh.

If you plan on visiting the Sacre-Coeur Basilica, consider taking a walk around Montmartre and visiting the Place du Tertre, where local artists display their work. Then, you can either take the funicular or climb the steps to the basilica and enjoy the view from the top.

Sainte-Chapelle

Located on the Île de la Cité, the Sainte-Chapelle is a masterpiece of Gothic architecture. It was built in the 13th century by King Louis IX to house the Crown of Thorns, and it is renowned for its stunning stained glass windows.

The chapel is divided into two levels: the lower chapel, which was used by the palace staff, and the upper chapel, which was reserved for the king and his close associates. The upper chapel is particularly impressive, with 15 large windows that fill the space with colorful light.

Visiting the Sainte-Chapelle is like stepping into a jewel box. The stained glass windows depict biblical scenes in intricate detail, and the effect is breathtaking.

If you plan on visiting the Sainte-Chapelle, consider buying your tickets in advance to avoid the long lines. Also, don't forget to visit the nearby Conciergerie, a former royal palace and prison that is now a museum.

Day Trip to Giverny

Giverny, located about 75 kilometers northwest of Paris, is the former home of the famous impressionist painter, Claude Monet. The artist lived and worked here for 43 years, and the house and gardens have been carefully restored and are open to the public.

The highlight of a visit to Giverny is Monet's garden, which is divided into two parts: the Clos Normand, a flower garden in front of the house, and the Japanese-inspired water garden, which features the famous lily pond that inspired many of Monet's paintings.

Visiting Giverny is like stepping into one of Monet's paintings. The gardens are meticulously maintained and feature a wide variety of flowers, plants, and trees. It is a perfect spot for a romantic stroll or a leisurely afternoon.

If you plan on visiting Giverny, consider taking a guided tour, as it will provide you with more information about Monet's life and work. Also, don't forget to visit the Monet's house and the nearby Museum of Impressionisms. Giverny is easily accessible by train and makes for a perfect day trip from Paris.

Final Thoughts

Paris, the City of Love, is the perfect destination for couples looking for a romantic getaway or for anyone wishing to experience the romantic side of life. From its iconic landmarks and beautiful gardens to its charming streets and artistic heritage, Paris offers a wealth of romantic experiences.

In this chapter, we have explored some of the most romantic spots in Paris, but there are many more waiting to be discovered. Consider visiting the Luxembourg Gardens, taking a walk along the Canal Saint-Martin, or exploring the romantic streets of the Marais.

Ultimately, the most romantic experiences in Paris are the ones you create yourself. Whether it is sharing a kiss under the Eiffel Tower, taking a sunset cruise on the Seine, or simply strolling hand in hand through the streets of this beautiful city, Paris offers endless opportunities for romance.

Let yourself be inspired by the romance of Paris and create your own unforgettable memories in this magnificent city.

CHAPTER 4: MODERN PARIS 51

CHAPTER 4:
Modern Paris

In contrast to its historic landmarks and timeless charm, Paris is also a city that embraces the modern world. With its contemporary architecture, innovative cultural institutions, and vibrant urban spaces, Paris offers a glimpse into the future while still honoring its past.

In this chapter, we will explore some of the most iconic modern attractions in Paris, from world-renowned museums and cultural centers to bustling urban spaces and entertainment districts. Whether you are an art enthusiast, a science buff, or simply looking to experience a different side of Paris, these attractions are sure to captivate your imagination.

Centre Pompidou

The Centre Pompidou, located in the Beaubourg area of the 4th arrondissement, is one of Paris' most iconic modern buildings. Designed by architects Renzo Piano and Richard Rogers, the building is a celebration of modern architecture, with its exposed structure, colorful façade, and innovative design.

Inside, the Centre Pompidou is home to the Musée National d'Art Moderne, one of the largest modern art museums in the world. Its collection includes works by artists such as Picasso, Matisse, and Duchamp.

In addition to the museum, the Centre Pompidou also houses a public library, a cinema, and a music and acoustics research center. Its rooftop terrace offers stunning views of the Paris skyline.

If you plan on visiting the Centre Pompidou, consider purchasing your tickets in advance to avoid the long lines. Also, don't forget to check out the nearby Stravinsky Fountain, a colorful and whimsical public art installation.

La Villette Park

Located in the 19th arrondissement, the Parc de la Villette is one of the largest parks in Paris. It was designed by architect Bernard Tschumi as a modern urban space that combines nature, architecture, and culture.

The park is home to several modern attractions, including the Cité des Sciences et de l'Industrie, a science museum that is perfect for both kids and adults, and the Philharmonie de Paris, a modern concert hall designed by Jean Nouvel.

In addition to its modern attractions, the Parc de la Villette also features themed gardens, playgrounds, and open spaces for picnics and outdoor activities. During the summer, the park hosts open-air concerts and film screenings.

If you plan on visiting the Parc de la Villette, consider bringing a picnic and spending the day exploring its various attractions. Also, don't forget to check out the nearby Canal de l'Ourcq, a picturesque waterway that is perfect for a leisurely stroll or a boat ride.

La Défense

La Défense, located in the western part of the Paris Metropolitan Area, is Europe's largest purpose-built business district. It is a showcase of modern architecture and urban planning, with its towering skyscrapers, open spaces, and contemporary sculptures. The most iconic structure in La Défense is the Grande Arche, a modern interpretation of the Arc de Triomphe, designed by Danish architect Johann Otto von Spreckelsen.

While La Défense is primarily a business district, there's plenty to see and do for visitors. Wander around the Parvis de la Défense, the vast pedestrian plaza at the heart of the district, take a ride to the top of the Grande Arche for panoramic views of Paris, or visit the open-air museum, which features over 60 sculptures by artists such as Calder, Miro, and César.

As La Défense is a bit out of the way from the central Paris attractions, plan your visit accordingly. The best way to get there is by taking Line 1 of the Paris Metro to La Défense station.

Arab World Institute

The Arab World Institute (Institut du Monde Arabe) is a cultural institute in Paris dedicated to the Arab world, its culture, and civilization. It is located in the 5th arrondissement on the left bank of the Seine River. Designed by a group of architects led by Jean Nouvel, the building is a remarkable example of modern architecture, featuring a façade of geometric patterns that change with the light and the time of day.

Inside, the institute houses a museum, a library, and an auditorium. The museum's collection includes a wide range of artifacts from the Arab world, from ancient manuscripts and ceramics to contemporary art and multimedia installations.

In addition to its permanent collection, the Arab World Institute also hosts temporary exhibitions, concerts, and lectures. Its rooftop terrace offers stunning views of the Notre-Dame Cathedral and the Paris skyline.

If you plan on visiting the Arab World Institute, consider checking its website for the current exhibitions and events. Also, don't forget to visit the rooftop terrace for a panoramic view of the city.

Orsay Museum

While the Musée d'Orsay is housed in a Beaux-Arts railway station built in the 1900s, its interior has been modernized and transformed into one of the world's most renowned art museums. Located on the left bank of the Seine River, opposite the Tuileries Gardens, the museum features an extensive collection of Impressionist and Post-Impressionist masterpieces by artists such as Monet, Van Gogh, Degas, and many others.

In addition to its famous paintings, the museum also houses a collection of sculptures, decorative arts, and photography. Its large clock window overlooking the Seine and the city is an iconic and popular spot for photographs.

If you plan on visiting the Musée d'Orsay, consider purchasing your tickets in advance to avoid the long lines. Also, don't forget to check out the museum's calendar for temporary exhibitions and special events.

Palais de Tokyo

The Palais de Tokyo is a contemporary art museum located in the 16th arrondissement, near the Trocadéro Gardens and the Seine River. It is housed in a modernist building that was originally constructed for the 1937 International Exposition.

Inside, the museum features a constantly changing program of exhibitions and events by contemporary artists from around the world. The museum's interior space is raw and unfinished, providing a unique backdrop for the art on display.

In addition to its exhibitions, the Palais de Tokyo also hosts performances, screenings, and workshops. Its bookstore is a great place to find art books and unique souvenirs.

If you plan on visiting the Palais de Tokyo, consider checking its website for the current exhibitions and events. Also, don't forget to explore the surrounding area, including the nearby Trocadéro Gardens and the Seine River.

Paris Philharmonic

The Philharmonie de Paris, commonly referred to as the Paris Philharmonic, is a cultural institution dedicated to music, located in the Parc de la Villette in the 19th arrondissement. Designed by the renowned architect Jean Nouvel, the building is a modern architectural marvel, with its innovative design and shiny metallic exterior.

The main concert hall of the Philharmonic is designed to provide excellent acoustics and a close connection between the artists and the audience. It hosts a wide range of musical performances, from classical music concerts to jazz and world music. In addition to concerts, the Philharmonic also offers educational programs, workshops, and exhibitions. Its rooftop terrace offers a panoramic view of Paris and is a great spot to relax before or after a concert. If you plan on attending a concert at the Paris Philharmonic, consider purchasing your tickets in advance, as many performances sell out quickly. Also, don't forget to visit the rooftop terrace for a stunning view of the city.

Science and Industry Museum

The Cité des Sciences et de l'Industrie, or the City of Science and Industry, is the largest science museum in Europe, located in the Parc de la Villette in the 19th arrondissement. The museum is housed in a modern building designed by the architect Adrien Fainsilber and features a range of interactive exhibits on various scientific and technological topics.

The museum's exhibits are designed to be engaging and accessible to people of all ages and backgrounds. They cover a wide range of topics, from astronomy and physics to biology and environmental science. The museum also features a planetarium, an IMAX theater, and a submarine that can be visited.

If you plan on visiting the City of Science and Industry, consider purchasing your tickets in advance to avoid the long lines. Also, don't forget to check out the museum's calendar for special events and temporary exhibitions.

Bercy Village

Bercy Village is a shopping and entertainment complex located in the 12th arrondissement, near the Seine River. It is housed in a series of restored wine warehouses from the 19th century and features a range of shops, restaurants, and cafes.

The cobblestone streets and historic buildings of Bercy Village provide a charming backdrop for a leisurely afternoon of shopping or dining. The complex also features a cinema and several art galleries.

In the summer months, Bercy Village hosts outdoor concerts and events, making it a lively and vibrant destination. It is located near the Parc de Bercy, a beautiful modern park that is worth a visit as well.

If you plan on visiting Bercy Village, consider combining it with a visit to the Parc de Bercy or a walk along the Seine River. Also, don't forget to check out the village's calendar for special events and concerts.

Fondation Louis Vuitton

The Fondation Louis Vuitton is a contemporary art museum and cultural center located in the Bois de Boulogne in the 16th arrondissement. Designed by the famous architect Frank Gehry, the building itself is a masterpiece of modern architecture, with its curvaceous glass panels and sail-like structures.

The museum's collection includes works by some of the most renowned contemporary artists from around the world. In addition to its permanent collection, the Fondation Louis Vuitton also hosts temporary exhibitions, concerts, and other cultural events.

The museum also features a restaurant and a bookstore, as well as terraces that offer stunning views of Paris and the Bois de Boulogne.

If you plan on visiting the Fondation Louis Vuitton, consider purchasing your tickets in advance to avoid the long lines. Also, don't forget to explore the terraces for panoramic views of the city.

Day Trip to Disneyland Paris

For those seeking a bit of modern magic, Disneyland Paris is the perfect day trip from the city center. Located in Marne-la-Vallée, about 35 kilometers east of Paris, Disneyland Paris is the most visited theme park in Europe.

The resort features two main parks: Disneyland Park, with its iconic Sleeping Beauty Castle, and Walt Disney Studios Park, dedicated to the world of cinema and animation. Both parks offer a range of attractions, shows, and parades that will delight visitors of all ages.

In addition to the parks, Disneyland Paris also features hotels, restaurants, and shops, making it a comprehensive entertainment destination.

If you plan on visiting Disneyland Paris, consider purchasing your tickets in advance to avoid the long lines. Also, don't forget to check out the resort's calendar for special events and seasonal celebrations.

Final Thoughts

In this chapter, we have explored some of the most modern and exciting sites in Paris, from the innovative architecture of the Fondation Louis Vuitton and the Centre Pompidou to the technological wonders of the City of Science and Industry and the magical world of Disneyland Paris.

However, this is just a small selection of the many modern attractions that Paris has to offer. The city is also home to numerous other contemporary art galleries, museums, and architectural marvels.

Moreover, Paris is constantly evolving, with new attractions and developments popping up all the time. So whether you are a fan of contemporary art, architecture, or just looking for a bit of modern entertainment, Paris has something to offer.

We hope this chapter has inspired you to explore the modern side of Paris and discover the many wonders that this ever-evolving city has to offer. Bon voyage!

CHAPTER 5:
Artistic Paris

Paris, a city synonymous with art and culture, has been a mecca for artists for centuries. From the Impressionists who painted its streets and riverbanks, to the modernists who revolutionized the art world, many of the world's most famous artists have called Paris home.

Today, the city continues to be a thriving center for the arts, boasting a vast array of museums, galleries, and street art. In this chapter, we will guide you through some of the artistic treasures that Paris has to offer, from its world-renowned museums to its hidden gems.

Louvre Museum

We have already discussed the Louvre Museum in general, but we would be remiss if we did not delve a little deeper into some of the specific works of art that make this museum a must-visit for any art lover.

One of the most famous paintings in the Louvre, and indeed the world, is Leonardo da Vinci's 'Mona Lisa.' This iconic portrait is known for the sitter's enigmatic smile and is a must-see for any visitor to the museum. Another must-see is Eugène Delacroix's 'Liberty Leading the People,' a powerful depiction of the July Revolution of 1830.

Additionally, the 'Winged Victory of Samothrace,' a stunning marble sculpture that stands at the top of a staircase in the museum, is another piece that should not be missed. The sheer scale and intricacy of this Hellenistic sculpture is breathtaking, and it is widely considered to be one of the greatest master-pieces of Hellenistic sculpture.

Orangerie Museum

The Musée de l'Orangerie is another must-visit museum for art lovers in Paris. Located in the Tuileries Gardens, this museum is home to a collection of Impressionist and Post-Impressionist paintings.

The museum is perhaps most famous for being the permanent home of eight large Water Lilies murals by Claude Monet, displayed in two oval rooms designed by the artist himself. These paintings are some of Monet's most famous works and seeing them in person is a truly unforgettable experience.

In addition to the Monet murals, the Orangerie Museum also houses works by other famous artists such as Pierre-Auguste Renoir, Henri Matisse, and Pablo Picasso. A visit to this museum offers a unique opportunity to see works by some of the greatest artists of the 20th century in a beautiful and serene setting.

Picasso Museum

The Musée Picasso, located in the Marais district, is dedicated to the life and work of Spanish artist Pablo Picasso. This museum is housed in the Hôtel Salé, a grand 17th-century mansion, and holds one of the most comprehensive collections of Picasso's works in the world.

The collection includes more than 5,000 pieces of art, encompassing paintings, sculptures, ceramics, prints, textiles, and drawings. Notable works include 'Self-Portrait' (1901), 'The Two Brothers' (1906), and 'Man with a Guitar' (1911). The museum also holds a vast archive of the artist's personal documents, photographs, and correspondence.

A visit to the Musée Picasso is not just a journey through the artist's creative evolution, but also a glimpse into his personal life, his relationships, and his political beliefs. It's an essential visit for anyone interested in 20th-century art and the life of one of its most influential figures.

Montmartre Artists Square

The Place du Tertre, commonly known as the Artists Square, is located in the Montmartre district of Paris. This small, bustling square is famous for its artists who set up their easels and paint en plein air, much like the artists of the past.

Montmartre has a long history as the haunt of artists and has been home to many famous painters including Picasso, Van Gogh, and Toulouse-Lautrec. Today, the Artists Square continues this tradition and is a great place to pick up a piece of original art or have your portrait painted.

While the area has become quite touristy, it still retains its bohemian charm and is a wonderful place to spend an afternoon. Wander the narrow streets, visit the art studios, and enjoy a coffee in one of the many cafes that line the square. It's a slice of artistic Paris that has remained largely unchanged for over a century.

Musée Marmottan Monet

The Musée Marmottan Monet, located in the 16th arrondissement of Paris, is home to the largest collection of works by Claude Monet in the world. This museum, originally a hunting lodge, was donated to the Académie des Beaux-Arts in 1932 and transformed into a museum dedicated to the works of the Impressionist painters.

The collection includes over 300 works by Monet, including some of his most famous pieces such as 'Impression, Sunrise' (the painting that gave Impressionism its name) and 'Water Lilies'. In addition to Monet, the museum also houses works by other Impressionist and Post-Impressionist artists such as Berthe Morisot, Edgar Degas, and Pierre-Auguste Renoir.

Visiting the Musée Marmottan Monet is like stepping back in time to the height of the Impressionist movement. The museum is set in a beautiful building and the artworks are displayed in a way that allows you to fully appreciate their beauty. It's a must-visit for any art lover visiting Paris.

Art Galleries in Le Marais

Le Marais, one of Paris' oldest and most charming neighborhoods, is a hub for art and culture. The district is home to many art galleries, ranging from small independent spaces to larger, more established venues.

The galleries in Le Marais feature a wide variety of art, from contemporary and modern pieces to classical paintings and sculptures. Some notable galleries include the Galerie Thaddaeus Ropac, which focuses on contemporary art, and the Galerie Perrotin, known for its exhibitions of emerging artists.

Exploring the art galleries in Le Marais is a great way to spend an afternoon in Paris. The district itself is a work of art, with its narrow cobblestone streets, historic buildings, and trendy boutiques and cafes. Take your time wandering around, popping into galleries that catch your eye, and soaking up the atmosphere of this vibrant neighborhood.

Street Art in Belleville

Belleville, a multicultural and bohemian neighborhood in Paris, is a hotspot for street art. The area is home to many artists and has a strong tradition of graffiti and street art.

As you walk through the streets of Belleville, you'll see colorful murals, intricate stencils, and thought-provoking paste-ups. Some pieces are by well-known artists, while others are by up-and-coming talents.

A guided tour of the street art in Belleville is a great way to learn more about the artists and the messages behind their work. However, you can also explore on your own, armed with a camera and a keen eye for detail.

Musée de Montmartre

The Musée de Montmartre is located in one of the oldest buildings in the Montmartre district and is dedicated to the history and culture of this iconic neighborhood.

The museum features a collection of paintings, posters, and memorabilia that tell the story of Montmartre, from its days as a rural village to its transformation into the bohemian enclave that attracted artists like Picasso, Van Gogh, and Toulouse-Lautrec.

One of the highlights of the Musée de Montmartre is the Renoir Gardens, which were once the studio of the famous painter Pierre-Auguste Renoir. The gardens are a peaceful oasis in the middle of the bustling city and offer stunning views of the Sacré-Cœur Basilica.

A visit to the Musée de Montmartre is a great way to learn more about the history of this fascinating neighborhood and the artists who called it home.

Musée national Gustave Moreau

The Musée national Gustave Moreau is dedicated to the works of the Symbolist painter Gustave Moreau. Located in the 9th arrondissement of Paris, the museum is housed in the artist's former residence and studio.

The collection includes over 1,300 paintings, drawings, and watercolors by Moreau, as well as sculptures and personal items that belonged to the artist. The museum is arranged on three floors, with the ground floor featuring Moreau's personal apartments, the first floor dedicated to his finished works, and the second floor showcasing his sketches and studies.

A visit to the Musée national Gustave Moreau offers a unique insight into the artist's creative process and is a must-see for fans of Symbolist art. Be sure to check out the museum's temporary exhibitions, which often feature works by other artists influenced by Moreau.

Musée Jacquemart-André

The Musée Jacquemart-André is located in a magnificent 19th-century mansion in the 8th arrondissement of Paris. The museum houses the collection of Edouard André and Nélie Jacquemart, a wealthy couple who were avid art collectors.

The collection includes a wide range of artworks, from Italian Renaissance paintings to 18th-century French decorative arts. Some highlights of the museum include works by Rembrandt, Botticelli, and Fragonard.

In addition to the permanent collection, the Musée Jacquemart-André also hosts temporary exhibitions, often focusing on a specific artist or period. Be sure to visit the museum's café, located in the former dining room of the mansion, for a cup of tea and a slice of cake.

Final Thoughts

Paris, often hailed as the art capital of the world, is home to an incredible array of art museums and galleries. From the world-famous Louvre Museum to the lesser-known Musée de Montmartre, there is something for every art lover in the city.

In this chapter, we have highlighted just a few of the many artistic treasures that Paris has to offer. However, the city is home to many more museums and galleries, each with its own unique collection and story to tell. We encourage you to explore beyond the beaten path and discover the lesser-known artistic gems of Paris.

As you wander through the city's streets, you'll also come across many examples of street art, from colorful murals to intricate stencils. Paris is a living art gallery, and there is always something new to discover around every corner.

We hope this guide has inspired you to explore the artistic side of Paris and to seek out the works of art that speak to you. Whether you're a fan of classical paintings or contemporary street art, Paris has something to offer you.

CHAPTER 6:
Parisian Cuisine

Paris, the capital of France, is not only renowned for its art, history, and romance, but it is also the epicenter of French cuisine. Parisian cuisine is an integral part of the city's culture, from its delectable pastries and artisanal cheeses to its world-class restaurants and cozy bistros.

In this chapter, we will take you on a culinary journey through Paris, exploring the city's most iconic dishes, its food markets, and even its cooking classes. Whether you are a foodie looking for the best croissant in town or a traveler eager to try something new, this guide will help you navigate the delicious world of Parisian cuisine.

French Pastries

France is famous for its pastries, and Paris is the best place to indulge in these sweet treats. From the flaky croissants and buttery pains au chocolat to the delicate macarons and decadent éclairs, Paris is a haven for pastry lovers.

One of the most iconic Parisian pastries is the croissant, a buttery, flaky, and delicious crescent-shaped pastry that is perfect for breakfast or a mid-morning snack. Another must-try is the macaron, a delicate almond meringue cookie filled with a layer of buttercream or ganache.

Paris is home to many world-renowned patisseries, such as Pierre Hermé and Ladurée, where you can enjoy these and many other pastries. However, don't overlook the smaller, lesser-known bakeries scattered throughout the city. Often, these local spots offer pastries that are just as delicious, if not more so, than those found in the more famous establishments.

Cheese and Wine

French cheese and wine are a match made in heaven, and Paris is the perfect place to enjoy this delightful pairing. France is home to over 1,000 different types of cheese, and many of them can be found in the cheese shops of Paris.

When it comes to wine, France is one of the world's largest producers, and Paris is home to many wine bars and shops where you can sample a wide variety of French wines. Whether you prefer a robust red, a crisp white, or a refreshing rosé, you'll find plenty of options to choose from.

For a truly Parisian experience, visit a local fromagerie to select some cheese, then head to a wine shop to pick up a bottle of wine. Finally, find a cozy spot in a park or along the Seine River to enjoy your picnic. Alternatively, many Parisian restaurants offer cheese and wine pairings on their menus, which can be a great way to try a variety of different combinations.

Haute Cuisine

Paris is renowned for its haute cuisine, a style of cooking that emphasizes the use of high-quality ingredients, meticulous preparation, and artistic presentation. The city is home to many

Michelin-starred restaurants, where chefs create innovative and delicious dishes that are a feast for both the eyes and the palate. One of the most famous Michelin-starred restaurants in Paris is Le Meurice, located in the luxurious Hotel Meurice. The restaurant, overseen by chef Alain Ducasse, offers a menu that combines traditional French cuisine with modern techniques and flavors.

Another notable restaurant is L'Ambroisie, located in the historic Place des Vosges. This three-Michelin-starred restaurant is known for its classic French cuisine and elegant ambiance.

While dining at a Michelin-starred restaurant is a memorable experience, it can also be quite expensive. Fortunately, there are many other restaurants in Paris that offer excellent haute cuisine at more affordable prices. For example, Le Comptoir du Relais, located in the Saint-Germain neighborhood, offers a prix fixe menu that is both delicious and reasonably priced.

Street Food

Paris may be known for its haute cuisine, but it also has a thriving street food scene. From savory crêpes and falafel to freshly baked baguettes and pastries, there are plenty of delicious options to choose from when you're on the go.

One of the most popular street food items in Paris is the crêpe, a thin pancake that can be filled with a variety of sweet or savory ingredients. For a classic Parisian experience, try a crêpe filled with Nutella and bananas or ham and cheese.

Another must-try street food item is falafel. The Marais neighborhood, in particular, is known for its excellent falafel stands. L'As du Fallafel is a popular spot that is often recommended by locals and visitors alike.

Don't forget to try a classic French baguette, which can be found at any boulangerie in the city. The baguette, a long, thin loaf of French bread, is a staple in Parisian cuisine and is perfect for making sandwiches or for enjoying with cheese and wine.

Cafés and Bistros

Cafés and bistros are an integral part of Parisian culture, and spending time in one of these establishments is a quintessential Parisian experience. Whether you're looking to enjoy a leisurely cup of coffee, a glass of wine, or a simple meal, there are plenty of options to choose from.

Cafés are typically open throughout the day and offer a relaxed environment where you can enjoy a cup of coffee, a light snack, or a casual meal. Many cafés also have outdoor seating, which is perfect for people-watching and enjoying the Parisian street scene.

Bistros, on the other hand, are small, informal restaurants that offer simple, hearty meals at reasonable prices. A typical bistro menu might include classic French dishes such as coq au vin, beef bourguignon, or escargot.

For a traditional Parisian café experience, visit Café de Flore, one of the city's oldest and most famous cafés. Located in the Saint-Germain neighborhood, Café de Flore has been a favorite hangout for artists, writers, and intellectuals for decades.

Another iconic café is Les Deux Magots, also located in Saint-Germain. Like Café de Flore, Les Deux Magots has a rich history and has been frequented by many famous figures, including Ernest Hemingway and Pablo Picasso.

Chocolate and Macarons

Paris is a haven for chocolate lovers, with countless chocolatiers scattered throughout the city, each offering their own unique creations. From rich and creamy milk chocolate to intense and flavorful dark chocolate, there is something for every taste.

One of the most famous chocolatiers in Paris is Pierre Hermé, who is often referred to as the 'Picasso of Pastry'. His shops offer a wide range of chocolates, macarons, and pastries, all of which are beautifully crafted and delicious.

Macarons, a type of meringue-based cookie filled with butter-cream or ganache, are another Parisian specialty. Ladurée is one of the most famous macaron shops in Paris and offers a wide variety of flavors, from classic vanilla and chocolate to more exotic options like rose and passion fruit.

While Ladurée and Pierre Hermé are two of the most well-known chocolatiers and macaron shops in Paris, there are many other excellent options to choose from. For example, Chocolat-erie Cyril Lignac is another popular spot that offers a range of delicious chocolates and pastries.

French Bread and Croissants

French bread and croissants are staples of Parisian cuisine and can be found in bakeries throughout the city. The baguette, a long, thin loaf of French bread, is perhaps the most iconic of all French breads. It is typically made with just four ingredients - flour, water, yeast, and salt - and is baked fresh every day.

Croissants are another popular pastry in Paris. These buttery, flaky pastries are typically enjoyed at breakfast or as a snack and can be found in virtually every bakery in the city.

For the best baguettes and croissants, it is worth seeking out a boulangerie that has been awarded the 'Meilleur Ouvrier de France' (MOF) designation. This is a prestigious award given to craftsmen in various trades, including baking, and is a sign of excellence.

Cooking Classes

For those looking to learn more about French cuisine and improve their cooking skills, there are many cooking schools in Paris that offer classes in English. These classes cover a wide range of topics, from classic French dishes to pastries and desserts.

Le Cordon Bleu, one of the most famous cooking schools in the world, offers a variety of classes in Paris. From one-day workshops to multi-week courses, there are options for cooks of all skill levels.

Another popular cooking school is L'Atelier des Chefs, which offers hands-on cooking classes in a relaxed and friendly environment. Classes are typically 90 minutes to two hours long and cover a wide range of topics, from basic cooking techniques to more advanced dishes.

Taking a cooking class is not only a fun and educational activity, but it also provides a unique opportunity to interact with local Parisians and learn about their culture and culinary traditions.

Food Markets

Paris is home to numerous food markets, offering a wide range of fresh produce, cheese, meat, fish, and other local products.

One of the most famous is the Marché Bastille, which is held on Thursdays and Sundays. Here, you can find everything from fresh fruits and vegetables to artisanal cheese and freshly baked bread.

Another popular market is the Marché d'Aligre, which is one of the oldest markets in Paris. It is open every day except Mondays and offers a wide variety of products, including fresh produce, flowers, and antiques.

Visiting a food market is a great way to experience the local culture and cuisine of Paris. It is also an opportunity to interact with local vendors and learn about the different products available.

Final Thoughts

Parisian cuisine is an integral part of the city's culture and history. From its world-renowned pastries and desserts to its artisanal cheese and wine, the culinary offerings of Paris are as diverse as they are delicious.

Whether you are a food lover looking to indulge in some of the finest cuisine in the world or a curious traveler looking to learn more about the local culture and traditions, Paris has something to offer for everyone.

Taking a cooking class, visiting a food market, or participating in a wine tasting are all unique and memorable experiences that will enrich your visit to Paris and provide you with a deeper understanding of the city and its people.

As you explore the culinary delights of Paris, don't forget to take the time to savor each bite and appreciate the artistry and craftsmanship that goes into each dish. Bon appétit!

CHAPTER 7:
Shopping in Paris

· ·

Paris is a shopper's paradise, offering a wide variety of shops, boutiques, and markets to explore. From high-end fashion boutiques to quirky vintage shops, and from iconic department stores to bustling flea markets, there's something for every taste and budget.

Shopping in Paris is not just a pastime, it's an experience. The city is home to some of the most famous fashion houses in the world, as well as a host of independent designers and artisans. Whether you're looking for the latest trends, timeless classics, or unique, one-of-a-kind pieces, you'll find it all in Paris.

In this chapter, we will guide you through some of the best shopping spots in Paris, from the famous to the hidden gems. Let's start our shopping adventure!

Flea Markets

One of the best ways to experience the local culture and find unique treasures is by visiting one of Paris's many flea markets. The most famous of these is the Marché aux Puces de Saint-Ouen, often simply referred to as Les Puces (The Fleas). Located in the north of the city, Les Puces is one of the largest flea markets in the world, covering seven hectares and featuring over 2,000 stalls.

Here, you'll find everything from vintage clothing and antique furniture to rare books and art. It's a great place to hunt for bargains, but also just to wander around and soak up the atmosphere. Remember to haggle, as it's all part of the experience!

Another popular flea market is the Marché aux Puces de la Porte de Vanves, which is located in the south of the city. It's smaller than Les Puces, but still offers a wide variety of items, from vintage postcards to antique jewelry.

Fashion Boutiques

Paris is the fashion capital of the world, and as such, it's home to a plethora of fashion boutiques. From iconic brands like Chanel and Louis Vuitton to independent designers, there's something for every fashion lover in Paris.

In the Marais district, you'll find a host of boutiques selling everything from cutting-edge fashion to vintage clothes. Rue des Rosiers and Rue Vieille du Temple are particularly good streets to explore.

Saint-Germain-des-Prés is another great area for shopping, with its mix of high-end boutiques and quirky independent shops. Boulevard Saint-Germain and Rue de Rennes are two of the main shopping streets in this area.

Don't forget to check out the boutiques in the trendy Canal Saint-Martin area, which is known for its hipster vibe and creative energy. Here, you'll find a host of independent designers selling everything from clothes and accessories to homeware and gifts.

Bookshops

Paris has a long and storied history with literature, being home to countless famous authors and the setting of many iconic novels. As a result, the city is dotted with many charming bookshops, each with its own unique character.

The most famous of these is Shakespeare and Company, located in the Latin Quarter. This historic bookshop has been a haunt of famous writers such as Ernest Hemingway, F. Scott Fitzgerald, and James Joyce. It's a must-visit for any book lover, not just for its literary history, but also for its quirky, cozy atmosphere.

Another notable bookshop is Librairie Galignani, located on Rue de Rivoli. It's one of the oldest English bookshops on the European continent and offers a wide range of English-language books.

For those interested in art books, Librairie 7L, located in the Saint-Germain-des-Prés district, is a great choice. This stylish bookshop is owned by fashion designer Karl Lagerfeld and offers a carefully curated selection of art, fashion, and design books.

Galleries Lafayette

The Galeries Lafayette is one of the most famous department stores in Paris and a must-visit for any shopaholic. Located on Boulevard Haussmann in the 9th arrondissement, it's a veritable temple of fashion, beauty, and gourmet food.

The store is housed in a stunning Belle Époque building, complete with a glass dome and an Art Nouveau staircase. Even if you're not planning on buying anything, it's worth a visit just for the architecture.

Of course, the main attraction here is the shopping. Galeries Lafayette offers a wide range of high-end brands, from fashion to cosmetics to accessories. There's also a gourmet food hall, featuring a selection of fine foods and wines.

Don't forget to visit the rooftop terrace, which offers stunning views over the city.

Le Marais Shops

Le Marais is one of the most fashionable districts in Paris and a great place to go shopping. The area is home to a wide range of shops, from high-end boutiques to quirky independent stores.

Rue des Francs-Bourgeois is one of the main shopping streets in Le Marais and offers a wide range of shops, from fashion to beauty to homeware. Another notable street is Rue de Turenne, which is home to many high-end boutiques and galleries.

Le Marais is also home to many vintage shops, offering everything from clothes and accessories to furniture and decorative items. Free'P'Star and Vintage Desir are two popular vintage shops in the area.

If you're looking for unique, handmade items, Le Marais is also home to many artisan shops. From jewelry and accessories to homeware and gifts, you'll find a wide range of handmade items in the area.

Antique Shops

For those who love antiques, Paris is a paradise. The city is home to many antique shops, each offering a treasure trove of unique and beautiful items. From furniture and art to jewelry and collectibles, you'll find a wide range of antiques in Paris.

The Carré Rive Gauche, located in the 7th arrondissement, is one of the most famous antique shopping areas in Paris. It's home to over 100 antique shops, each offering a unique selection of items. Another notable antique shopping area is the Village Saint-Paul, located in the Marais. This charming area is home to many antique shops and galleries, all located in beautiful medieval buildings.

For those looking for a bargain, the Marché aux Puces de Saint-Ouen, located in the north of Paris, is a must-visit. It's one of the largest flea markets in the world and offers a wide range of items, from antiques and vintage clothing to books and records.

Day Trip to La Vallée Village

For those looking for designer items at discounted prices, a day trip to La Vallée Village is a must. Located about 35 kilometers east of Paris, near Disneyland Paris, La Vallée Village is a luxury outlet shopping village.

The village is home to over 120 boutiques, each offering a wide range of high-end brands at discounted prices. From fashion and accessories to homeware and beauty, you'll find a wide range of luxury items at La Vallée Village.

The village is beautifully designed, with charming streets and squares. There are also many cafés and restaurants, making it a great place to spend a day.

To get to La Vallée Village, you can take a train from Paris to Val d'Europe station, and then it's just a short walk to the village. Alternatively, there are also shuttle buses that run from central Paris to La Vallée Village.

Final Thoughts

Shopping in Paris is a unique experience, offering a wide range of options from high-end boutiques and department stores to quirky independent shops, vintage stores, and bustling markets. Whether you're looking for fashion, art, antiques, or gourmet food, you'll find it in Paris.

Remember to take a break from shopping to enjoy a coffee or a meal at one of the city's many cafés and restaurants. And don't forget to explore the charming streets and squares of the city, as they are full of hidden gems.

In conclusion, Paris offers a shopping experience like no other. With its wide range of shops, beautiful streets, and vibrant atmosphere, it's a city that will leave a lasting impression. Happy shopping!

CHAPTER 8:
Nightlife in Paris

Paris is famous for its vibrant nightlife, offering a wide range of options for both locals and visitors. From traditional cabarets and jazz clubs to modern rooftop bars and nightclubs, there is something for everyone in the City of Light. Whether you are looking for a relaxed evening with friends, a romantic night out, or a wild night of dancing, Paris has it all.

In this chapter, we will guide you through some of the best nightlife options in Paris, providing tips and recommendations to help you make the most of your evening.

So, put on your dancing shoes, and let's dive into the Parisian nightlife!

Cabarets and Shows

Paris is the birthplace of cabaret, a form of entertainment that combines music, dance, and drama. The city is home to many famous cabarets, including the Moulin Rouge, the Lido, and the Crazy Horse.

The Moulin Rouge, located in the Montmartre district, is the most famous cabaret in the world. It's known for its extravagant costumes, elaborate sets, and talented dancers. The Lido, located on the Champs-Elysées, is another iconic cabaret, known for its glamorous shows and beautiful dancers. The Crazy Horse, located near the Alma-Marceau metro station, is famous for its artistic and avant-garde performances.

If you're looking for a more traditional cabaret experience, consider visiting the Au Lapin Agile, a historic cabaret in Montmartre. It's been a favorite haunt of artists and writers for over a century and offers a cozy and intimate atmosphere.

When visiting a cabaret in Paris, it's advisable to book your tickets in advance, as shows often sell out. Also, most cabarets have a dress code, so be sure to check this before you go.

Jazz Clubs

Paris has a rich jazz history and is home to many renowned jazz clubs. The city played a significant role in the development of jazz music, and many famous jazz musicians, including Duke Ellington and Miles Davis, performed in Paris.

One of the most famous jazz clubs in Paris is the Caveau de la Huchette, located in the Latin Quarter. It's been a jazz club since the 1940s and has hosted many famous musicians over the years. Another iconic jazz club is the Duc des Lombards, located in the Châtelet area. It's one of the most popular jazz clubs in Paris and hosts live music every night.

For a more modern and trendy vibe, check out the New Morning, located in the 10th arrondissement. It's one of the largest jazz clubs in Paris and hosts a wide range of music, from jazz and blues to funk and soul.

Most jazz clubs in Paris have a cover charge, which usually includes your first drink. It's also advisable to book your table in advance, especially on weekends when the clubs can get very busy.

Rooftop Bars

Rooftop bars are a popular choice for those looking to enjoy a drink with a view. Paris has several rooftop bars that offer stunning views of the city skyline, making them a perfect spot for a romantic evening or a night out with friends.

One of the most famous rooftop bars in Paris is Le Perchoir, located in the 11th arrondissement. It offers panoramic views of the city, and is a popular spot for both locals and tourists. Another popular rooftop bar is the Terrass" Hotel, located in Montmartre. It offers stunning views of the Eiffel Tower and is a great spot to watch the sunset.

For a more upscale experience, consider visiting the rooftop bar at the Peninsula Hotel, located near the Arc de Triomphe. It offers a luxurious setting and breathtaking views of the city.

Most rooftop bars in Paris are open year-round, but it's always a good idea to check their opening hours and dress code before you go. Also, as they are very popular, it's advisable to book a table in advance.

Nightclubs

Paris has a vibrant nightclub scene, with clubs to suit all tastes and styles. Whether you are into electronic music, hip-hop, or Latin music, you will find a nightclub in Paris that plays your favorite tunes.

One of the most famous nightclubs in Paris is the Rex Club, located on the Grands Boulevards. It's one of the oldest and most respected clubs in the city and is known for its techno and electronic music. Another popular nightclub is the Showcase, located under the Pont Alexandre III. It's a unique venue set in a former boat hangar and hosts some of the biggest DJs in the world.

For those looking for a more glamorous nightclub experience, consider visiting the Matignon, located near the Champs-Elysées. It's a luxurious club with a chic and sophisticated atmosphere.

Most nightclubs in Paris have a cover charge, which usually includes your first drink. Also, many clubs have a strict dress code, so be sure to check this before you go.

Cinema and Film

Paris has a long history of cinema and is home to many historic theaters and film festivals. Whether you are a film buff or just looking for a relaxing way to spend an evening, watching a movie in Paris is a great option.

One of the most famous cinemas in Paris is the Cinémathèque Française, located in the 12th arrondissement. It's a film archive, museum, and theater all in one and hosts regular screenings of classic and contemporary films. Another iconic cinema is the Grand Rex, located on the Grands Boulevards. It's the largest cinema in Europe and is known for its Art Deco architecture and luxurious interior.

For a more intimate cinema experience, consider visiting one of the many independent cinemas in Paris, such as the Nouveau Latina in the Marais or the Studio 28 in Montmartre.

If you are in Paris during the spring, be sure to check out the Paris Film Festival, which showcases the best of international cinema. Also, during the summer months, there are several outdoor film screenings throughout the city, such as the Cinéma en Plein Air at the Parc de la Villette.

Final Thoughts

Paris, the city of lights, has a nightlife as vibrant and diverse as its day life. From its iconic cabarets and jazz clubs to its modern rooftop bars and nightclubs, there is something for everyone in Paris after dark.

The nightlife in Paris is not just about drinking and dancing, although there is plenty of that. It's also about enjoying the arts, whether it's watching a cabaret show, listening to live jazz, or catching a film at one of the city's historic cinemas. It's about experiencing the Parisian way of life, which includes taking the time to enjoy good food, good wine, and good company.

Also, remember that the nightlife in Paris starts later than in many other cities. Most Parisians don't head out until around 11 pm or midnight, and many places stay open until the early hours of the morning. So, take a nap in the afternoon, have a late dinner, and then head out to enjoy the Parisian night.

Lastly, don't forget to be respectful and mindful of others when you are out and about in Paris at night. Parisians take their nightlife seriously, and it's important to follow the local customs and etiquettes. For example, it's customary to greet others with a kiss on both cheeks, and it's considered rude to speak too loudly or to take photos without asking permission.

In conclusion, the nightlife in Paris offers a wide range of options for both locals and visitors. Whether you are looking for a quiet night out or a wild night of dancing, you will find it in Paris. So, put on your dancing shoes, grab a glass of wine, and head out to enjoy the Parisian night. Your adventure awaits!

CHAPTER 9:
Off the Beaten Path

· ·

Paris is a city that everyone wants to visit, but it's easy to get caught up in the tourist traps and miss out on the city's hidden gems. While the Eiffel Tower, Louvre, and Notre Dame are must-see attractions, there's a whole other side of Paris that many tourists never get to experience. This chapter will guide you to some off the beaten path locations in Paris that will give you a different perspective of the city and help you to discover its lesser-known treasures.

Canal Saint-Martin

The Canal Saint-Martin is a 4.6 km long canal located in the 10th and 11th arrondissements of Paris. It connects the Canal de l'Ourcq to the river Seine. Built during the 19th century under the orders of Napoleon Bonaparte, it was originally designed to provide the city with fresh water. Today, it's a popular spot for both locals and tourists, although it remains relatively unexplored by the majority of the latter.

The area surrounding the canal is trendy and bohemian, with an array of independent shops, boutiques, cafes, and bars. During the summer months, the canal banks are filled with Parisians enjoying picnics, playing music, or simply relaxing with friends. It's a great place to take a leisurely walk and observe local life.

For a unique experience, consider taking a canal cruise. It offers a different view of Paris and allows you to pass through several locks and under beautiful iron footbridges. The cruise usually takes around two and a half hours and is a relaxing way to see a different side of the city.

La Campagne à Paris

La Campagne à Paris is a small, picturesque neighborhood located in the 20th arrondissement. It's a hidden oasis that many tourists, and even some Parisians, are unaware of. The area consists of small houses with gardens, which is a rarity in Paris. The houses were built at the beginning of the 20th century for working-class Parisians, but today they are highly sought after and have become quite expensive.
Walking through La Campagne à Paris feels like stepping into a small village rather than being in a bustling metropolis. The narrow streets, cobblestone pathways, and charming houses make it a perfect spot for a leisurely stroll and for taking photos. To get there, take the metro to the Porte de Bagnolet station and then it's just a short walk to the neighborhood. It's worth the effort to visit this hidden gem and experience a side of Paris that few get to see.

Les Arènes de Lutèce

Les Arènes de Lutèce, located in the 5th arrondissement, is one of the most hidden historical sites in Paris. It is the remnants of a Roman amphitheater that could once hold up to 15,000 spectators. Built in the 1st century AD, it was used for various performances, gladiatorial combats, and other public spectacles.

Today, it's a public park where locals come to relax and children play. While the majority of the amphitheater has been destroyed over time, some of the original structure, including parts of the stage and the tiered seating, can still be seen.

Visiting Les Arènes de Lutèce gives you a glimpse into the ancient history of Paris, and it's fascinating to think about what events took place there over 2000 years ago. It's also a peaceful oasis in the middle of the city and a great spot for a picnic.

Parc de Bercy

Parc de Bercy is located in the 12th arrondissement, on the right bank of the Seine River. It is one of the most modern parks in Paris and is divided into three different gardens: the Romantic Garden, which features fishponds and dunes; the Flowerbeds, home to a variety of plants and trees; and the Meadows, an open space perfect for picnics and relaxation.

The park also features a vineyard, which is a reminder of the area's past as a wine market. In addition, there is a series of themed gardens, sculptures, and water features that make it a pleasant place to take a walk.

Adjacent to the park is the modern Bercy Village, a shopping and dining area located in renovated wine warehouses. It's a great place to grab a meal or do some shopping after a walk in the park.

Musée de la Chasse et de la Nature

The Musée de la Chasse et de la Nature, located in the Marais district, is one of the most unusual museums in Paris. It is dedicated to hunting and nature, and its collection includes a wide variety of hunting equipment, trophies, and artworks related to hunting and nature.

The museum is housed in two beautiful mansions, the Hôtel de Guénégaud and the Hôtel de Mongelas. The interior of the museum is richly decorated and features wood paneling, chandeliers, and antique furniture. The exhibits are displayed in a way that creates a dialogue between art and nature.

Visiting the Musée de la Chasse et de la Nature offers a unique perspective on the relationship between humans and the natural world. It's also a chance to see some beautiful and unusual artworks, including paintings, sculptures, and tapestries.

Little Tokyo

Little Tokyo in Paris is not an official district, but rather a nickname given to a small area in the 1st arrondissement, near the Palais Royal and the Louvre. This area is home to a concentration of Japanese restaurants, bakeries, supermarkets, and bookshops, making it the go-to place for Japanese culture and cuisine in Paris.

Walking through the streets of Little Tokyo, you'll find sushi bars, ramen shops, and Japanese grocery stores. There are also several Japanese bakeries selling delicious pastries and sweets. If you're a fan of manga and anime, there are bookshops selling a wide variety of Japanese comics and DVDs.

Visiting Little Tokyo is like taking a short trip to Japan without leaving Paris. It's a great place to grab a meal, do some shopping, or just take a walk and soak in the atmosphere.

Chinatown

Paris has several Chinatowns, but the largest and most well-known is located in the 13th arrondissement. This area is home to a large population of Asian residents, and the streets are lined with Chinese, Vietnamese, and Cambodian restaurants, supermarkets, and shops.

One of the main attractions in this Chinatown is the Tang Frères supermarket, which is one of the largest Asian supermarkets in Paris. It's a great place to buy exotic fruits, vegetables, spices, and other ingredients that can be hard to find elsewhere in the city.

Another highlight of this area is the annual Chinese New Year parade, which is one of the most colorful and festive events in Paris. The streets are filled with dragon and lion dances, martial arts performances, and traditional Chinese music.

Belleville and Ménilmontant

Belleville and Ménilmontant are two neighboring districts located in the 20th arrondissement, in the east of Paris. These areas have a diverse and bohemian atmosphere, with a mix of cultures and a strong artistic community.

Belleville is home to one of the largest Chinese communities in Paris, and there are many Asian restaurants and shops in the area. It's also known for its street art, and there are several streets where you can see large murals and graffiti art. Belleville Park offers a panoramic view of the city, and it's a great place to take a walk and enjoy the scenery.

Ménilmontant has a more village-like atmosphere, with narrow streets, small shops, and cafes. It's a popular area for nightlife, with many bars and live music venues. The cemetery of Père Lachaise, where many famous people are buried, is also located in this area.

Both Belleville and Ménilmontant are off the beaten path and offer a different perspective on Paris. They are great places to explore if you want to get away from the tourist crowds and experience a more authentic side of the city.

La Petite Ceinture

The Petite Ceinture, or "Little Belt," is a former railway line that circles Paris. Built in the 19th century, it was used for passenger and freight transportation until it was closed in the 1930s. Since then, it has been largely abandoned and overgrown, creating a unique urban wilderness in the heart of the city.

In recent years, parts of the Petite Ceinture have been opened to the public as a walking trail. The trail offers a unique perspective on Paris, passing through tunnels, over bridges, and along elevated sections with views over the city. The path is lined with wildflowers and shrubs, and it's a popular spot for birdwatching. Walking along the Petite Ceinture is like stepping back in time. The old railway tracks, stations, and infrastructure are still in place, creating a nostalgic atmosphere. It's a great place for a leisurely walk or a jog, and it offers a different perspective on the city.

Day Trip to Vincennes Forest

The Bois de Vincennes is a large public park located on the eastern edge of Paris. It's the largest green space in the city, and it offers a wide range of outdoor activities, from boating and fishing to jogging and cycling.

One of the main attractions in the park is the Château de Vincennes, a medieval castle that was once a hunting lodge for the French kings. The castle is surrounded by a moat and has a large keep, a chapel, and a drawbridge. It's a great place to explore and learn about the history of the area.

The Parc Floral de Paris is another highlight of the Bois de Vincennes. It's a beautiful botanical garden with a wide variety of plants and flowers. There are also several lakes and ponds in the park, where you can rent a boat or just sit and enjoy the scenery.

The Bois de Vincennes is a great place to escape the hustle and bustle of the city and enjoy some fresh air and nature. It's easily accessible by metro or bus, and it's a great place for a day trip or a picnic.

Final Thoughts

Exploring off the beaten path in Paris can lead to some unexpected and delightful discoveries. From the urban wilderness of the Petite Ceinture to the diverse neighborhoods of Belleville and Ménilmontant, there are plenty of hidden gems to discover in the City of Light.

In addition to the places mentioned in this chapter, there are many other lesser-known attractions in Paris. For example, the Musée des Arts Forains is a museum dedicated to fairground art, and the Parc des Buttes-Chaumont is a beautiful park with a large lake and a temple on a hill.

There are also many interesting neighborhoods to explore, such as the Canal Saint-Martin, with its trendy boutiques and cafes, and the Marais, with its narrow streets and historic buildings.

Overall, venturing off the beaten path in Paris is a rewarding experience that offers a different perspective on the city. It's a great way to see a more authentic side of Paris and discover places that most tourists never get to see.

CHAPTER 10: PARIS THROUGH THE SEASONS   113

CHAPTER 10:
Paris Through the Seasons

Paris, the City of Light, is renowned for its art, gastronomy, and culture. With every season, the city transforms and brings with it a distinct ambiance, a new array of activities, and a unique palette of flavors. Spring blooms turn the city into a romantic haven, while summer brings out the liveliness and vibrancy of Paris. As the leaves change colors, autumn offers a cozy, nostalgic atmosphere, and winter wraps the city in a magical, festive spirit. This chapter will guide you through Paris in each season, ensuring you make the most of your visit no matter when you decide to travel.

Spring in Paris

Spring is often considered the best time to visit Paris. As the city shakes off the winter chill, flowers bloom, terraces fill up, and there's a sense of renewal in the air. Cherry blossoms paint the city in shades of pink and white, creating picturesque scenes at every turn.

▸ Cherry Blossom Viewing: One of the highlights of spring is the blooming of cherry blossoms. Notable spots for cherry blossom viewing include the Notre-Dame Cathedral, the Jardin des Plantes, and the Parc du Champ de Mars, where the iconic Eiffel Tower serves as a backdrop.

- ▶ Gardens and Parks: Spring is the perfect time to explore Paris' beautiful gardens and parks. The Jardin des Tuileries and Jardin du Luxembourg burst into color with blooming flowers and freshly trimmed lawns. It's the perfect time for a leisurely stroll or a picnic with friends and family.
- ▶ Spring Events and Festivals: Springtime in Paris also brings a host of events and festivals. The Foire du Trône, a funfair that dates back to 957, takes place from late March to late May. Also, the Nuit des Musées, or Night of Museums, is an event where museums across the city open their doors for free and host special events and exhibitions throughout the night.

Spring is a time of rejuvenation, making it an ideal season to explore the city, dine al fresco, and take part in outdoor activities. It is a season of hope and vibrancy that brings out the best in Paris.

Summer in Paris

Summer in Paris is marked by long, sunny days and a bustling atmosphere. Parisians and tourists alike take to the streets to enjoy the warmth, filling the city with a lively energy.

- ▶ Outdoor Activities: Summer is the perfect time for outdoor activities. Enjoy a Seine river cruise, take a bike tour of the city, or relax on the artificial beaches set up along the Seine during the Paris Plages event.
- ▶ Temporary Urban Beaches: Paris Plages is an annual event where sections of the Seine's banks are transformed

into temporary urban beaches, complete with sand, deck chairs, and palm trees. It's a great way to enjoy the summer sun without leaving the city.

▸ Summer Festivals and Events: Summer is also a time for festivals and events. Fête de la Musique, a music festival that takes place on the summer solstice, fills the streets with music of all genres. Bastille Day, on July 14th, is marked with a military parade on the Champs-Élysées, followed by fireworks at the Eiffel Tower.

Summer in Paris is a time of celebration and outdoor fun. It's a season of sunshine and warmth that encourages exploration and enjoyment of the city's many offerings. From cultural festivals to outdoor activities, summer in Paris is not to be missed.

Autumn in Paris

Autumn in Paris brings a cozy, nostalgic atmosphere. As the leaves change colors and the air turns crisp, the city takes on a different kind of beauty.

▸ Fall Foliage: Autumn is the perfect time to enjoy the fall foliage in Paris. The city's gardens and parks, such as the Bois de Boulogne and Parc des Buttes-Chaumont, become a riot of colors, with leaves turning shades of red, orange, and yellow.

▸ Wine Harvest: Autumn is also the time for grape harvesting and wine production. The Montmartre Grape Harvest Festival is a popular event that celebrates the grape harvest in the Montmartre vineyard. It includes a parade, concerts, and, of course, wine tasting.

▸ Cultural Events: Autumn is a busy season for cultural events in Paris. The Nuit Blanche, an annual all-night arts festival, takes place in October. Galleries, museums, and other cultural institutions open their doors for free, hosting special exhibitions and events throughout the night. Autumn in Paris is a time of cultural richness and natural beauty. It is a season of reflection and appreciation, making it an ideal time to explore the city's art and culture, enjoy its culinary delights, and take leisurely strolls through its beautiful parks and gardens.

Winter in Paris

Winter in Paris wraps the city in a magical, festive spirit. As the temperatures drop, the city lights up, creating a warm and cozy atmosphere.

▶ Christmas Markets: Winter is the time for Christmas markets in Paris. Wooden chalets selling handmade crafts, mulled wine, and seasonal treats line the streets, creating a festive atmosphere. The most famous Christmas market is held on the Champs-Élysées.

▶ Holiday Lights: The city is beautifully illuminated during the winter months. The holiday lights on the Champs-Élysées, the window displays at the Galeries Lafayette, and the sparkling lights on the Eiffel Tower create a magical atmosphere.

▶ Winter Sports: Ice skating is a popular winter activity in Paris. Several outdoor ice rinks open during the winter months, including one on the first floor of the Eiffel Tower.

Winter in Paris is a time of celebration and joy. It is a season of lights and festivity that brings a sense of magic to the city. From holiday markets to ice skating, winter in Paris offers a host of activities and events that are sure to make your visit memorable.

Dining Out

Dining in Paris is always a special experience, and each season offers its own unique flavors and settings.

- ▸ Spring: Spring is the perfect time to enjoy outdoor dining in Paris. Many restaurants and cafes open their terraces and gardens for al fresco dining. Enjoy a leisurely meal of fresh, seasonal produce while basking in the spring sunshine.
- ▸ Summer: In summer, the city comes alive with outdoor dining options. From rooftop terraces to riverside cafes, there are plenty of places to enjoy a meal in the open air. Don't miss the opportunity to try some delicious summer dishes like ratatouille or a refreshing gazpacho.
- ▸ Autumn: Autumn is the season for comfort food, and Parisian bistros are the perfect place to enjoy hearty, warming dishes. Try classics like coq au vin or boeuf bourguignon, and don't forget to pair your meal with a glass of red wine.
- ▸ Winter: Winter is the time for cozy, intimate dining. Many Parisian restaurants have fireplaces, creating a warm and inviting atmosphere. This is the time to enjoy rich, indulgent dishes like cassoulet or tartiflette.

Seasonal Shopping

Paris is a shopping paradise, and each season offers its own unique opportunities.

- ▸ Spring: Spring is a great time to update your wardrobe with the latest fashions. The winter sales are over, and shops are stocked with new collections. Don't miss the opportunity to shop for stylish spring clothing and accessories.

▶ Summer: Summer is the time for sales in Paris. The summer sales, or 'soldes', usually start in June and last for several weeks. This is the best time to snag a bargain on everything from clothes to homeware.

▶ Autumn: Autumn is the time to shop for warmer clothing and accessories. Parisian boutiques are filled with stylish coats, scarves, and hats. It's also a great time to shop for home decor items, as many stores have new collections in stock.

▶ Winter: Winter is the time for Christmas shopping in Paris. The city is filled with Christmas markets, and the shops are beautifully decorated for the holiday season. This is the time to shop for gifts, festive decorations, and seasonal treats.

Cultural Activities

Paris is a cultural hub, and there are always plenty of events and activities to enjoy, no matter the season.

▶ Spring: Spring is a busy time for art exhibitions in Paris. Many museums and galleries host special exhibitions to coincide with the arrival of spring. It's also a great time to enjoy outdoor concerts and performances.

▶ Summer: Summer is the season for festivals in Paris. From music festivals to open-air cinema screenings, there are plenty of cultural events to enjoy in the summer months.

▶ Autumn: Autumn is a great time to enjoy indoor cultural activities in Paris. The theatre season kicks off in autumn, and there are plenty of concerts, operas, and dance performances to enjoy.

- ► Winter: Winter is the time for festive cultural events in Paris. From Christmas concerts to Nutcracker ballet performances, there are plenty of ways to get into the holiday spirit. It's also a great time to visit the city's museums and galleries, as they are less crowded during the winter months.

Outdoor Activities

Paris offers a plethora of outdoor activities that vary with each season.

- ► Spring: Spring is the perfect time for picnics in Paris. The city's parks and gardens come alive with colorful flowers and greenery. Grab a baguette, some cheese, and a bottle of wine and head to a local park for a leisurely picnic. It's also a great time to take a boat tour of the Seine or rent a bike and explore the city.
- ► Summer: Summer is the perfect time to be outdoors in Paris. Take a walk along the Seine, rent a kayak, or enjoy a game of pétanque in one of the city's parks. Many parks also offer outdoor exercise classes, yoga sessions, and other activities.
- ► Autumn: Autumn is a great time to take a walk in the woods. The Bois de Boulogne and Bois de Vincennes are two large parks on the outskirts of Paris that offer plenty of walking trails. It's also a good time to take a hot air balloon ride and enjoy the fall foliage from above.
- ► Winter: Winter is the time for ice skating in Paris. Many of the city's squares and parks set up temporary ice rinks. It's also a great time to take a brisk walk along the Seine or visit one of the city's outdoor markets.

Festivals and Traditions

Paris is a city of traditions, and each season has its own special celebrations.

- Spring: Spring is the time for Easter celebrations in Paris. Many bakeries and patisseries offer special Easter treats, and there are Easter egg hunts in many of the city's parks. It's also the time for the Foire du Trône, a large funfair held in the Bois de Vincennes.
- Summer: Summer is the time for the Fête de la Musique, a city-wide music festival held on June 21st. It's also the time for Bastille Day celebrations on July 14th, complete with fireworks and a military parade.
- Autumn: Autumn is the time for the Nuit Blanche, an all-night arts festival held in October. It's also the time for the Montmartre Wine Harvest Festival, a celebration of the grape harvest in the Montmartre vineyard.
- Winter: Winter is the time for Christmas celebrations in Paris. The city is beautifully decorated, and there are Christmas markets, concerts, and other festive events. It's also the time for New Year's Eve celebrations.

Practical Tips

No matter what the season, there are a few practical tips to keep in mind when visiting Paris.

- Spring: Spring weather can be unpredictable, so it's best to dress in layers and bring a lightweight jacket. It's also a good idea to bring an umbrella, as spring showers are common.
- Summer: Summer in Paris can be hot, so it's best to wear light, breathable fabrics. Don't forget sunscreen, sunglasses, and a hat.

- Autumn: Autumn in Paris can be chilly, so it's best to wear warm clothes and bring a jacket. It's also a good idea to bring an umbrella, as autumn rains are common.
- Winter: Winter in Paris can be cold, so it's best to dress warmly and bring a coat, scarf, gloves, and hat. If you're planning on visiting outdoor attractions, it's also a good idea to bring a thermos with hot tea or coffee to keep warm.

Final Thoughts

As we conclude our journey through Paris across the seasons, it's clear that the City of Light has something special to offer at any time of the year. Whether it's the blooming flowers and picnics in the spring, the outdoor activities and festivals in the summer, the colorful foliage and art events in the fall, or the festive lights and Christmas markets in the winter, there is always something magical happening in Paris.

Each season has its own charm and unique activities, and it's worth visiting Paris in different seasons to experience them all. From the outdoor dining in spring and summer, to the seasonal shopping, cultural events, outdoor activities, festivals, and practical tips discussed, it's clear that a little planning can help you make the most of your visit, no matter when you decide to go.

In spring, the city wakes up from its winter slumber, and there is a sense of renewal in the air. The trees start to bud, flowers bloom, and the outdoor terraces of cafes and restaurants start to fill up. It's the perfect time for a leisurely picnic in one of Paris's beautiful parks or gardens, and to explore the city on foot or by bike.

Summer, on the other hand, is a time of celebration in Paris. The city is alive with music, art, and outdoor activities. It's the perfect time to explore the Seine River banks, enjoy the city's many festivals, and take in the lively atmosphere of the Parisian streets.

As the leaves start to change color, autumn brings a sense of nostalgia to Paris. It's a great time to explore the city's parks and gardens, enjoy its cultural offerings, and sample its delicious cuisine. The cooler temperatures make it perfect for long walks and sightseeing tours.

Winter in Paris is a magical time. The city is beautifully decorated for the holidays, and there is a festive atmosphere in the air. It's the perfect time to enjoy the Christmas markets, go ice skating, and take in the beautiful lights and decorations.

Ultimately, Paris is a city that can be enjoyed year-round. Each season brings its own unique charm and set of activities, making it a destination that invites repeated visits. Whether you're a lover of art, history, food, or just enjoying the great outdoors, Paris has something to offer you in every season.

Remember to plan ahead and adjust your activities to the season. Consider the practical tips we've discussed for dressing and packing appropriately, and be prepared to embrace the Parisian way of life, whatever the weather.

In closing, Paris is not just a destination, it's an experience that changes with the seasons. No matter when you choose to visit, there is always something new to discover, and a new memory to be made. Bon voyage!

CHAPTER 11:
How to Travel Paris on a Budget

Paris, often referred to as "The City of Love" or "The City of Lights," is a dream destination for many travelers around the world. Known for its world-class art, gastronomy, and culture, it's no wonder why so many people are drawn to this beautiful city.

However, it is also known for being quite expensive. Accommodation, dining, and attractions can quickly add up and make your trip much more costly than anticipated. But fear not! It is entirely possible to enjoy Paris on a budget. With a little bit of planning and some insider tips, you can make your money go further and still have a fantastic experience in the French capital.

Budget Accommodation

Accommodation is often one of the biggest expenses when traveling, and Paris is no exception. However, there are several budget-friendly options available if you know where to look. Hostels are a popular choice for budget travelers. They offer dormitory-style rooms with shared facilities, and many also have private rooms available for a slightly higher cost. Some popular and well-rated hostels in Paris include Generator Paris, St. Christopher's Inn, and MIJE Marais.

Another option for budget accommodation is to rent a private room or apartment through a vacation rental site like Airbnb or Booking.com. This can often be more cost-effective than staying in a hotel, especially if you are traveling with a group and can split the cost. Additionally, having access to a kitchen can help you save money on meals.

Eating on a Budget

Eating out in Paris can be quite expensive, but there are several ways to save money on meals. One of the best ways to eat on a budget is to visit local markets and buy fresh produce, cheese, and bread to make your own meals. There are many markets throughout the city, and they offer a wide variety of delicious and affordable food options.

Another way to save money on meals is to eat at cafés or bistros rather than more expensive restaurants. Many cafés offer a "plat du jour" or "dish of the day" at a reasonable price. Also, consider eating your main meal at lunchtime rather than dinner, as many restaurants offer lunch specials at a reduced price.

Don't forget to take advantage of the many delicious and affordable street food options in Paris. Crepes, falafel, and baguette sandwiches are all tasty and budget-friendly options. Additionally, many bakeries offer inexpensive quiches, sandwiches, and pastries that are perfect for a quick and cheap meal.

Public Transport

Public transportation is the most economical and efficient way to get around Paris. The city has an extensive public transportation system, including buses, trams, and the Métro (subway). A single ticket for the Métro or bus costs €1.90 (in 2023), and it is valid for a one-way journey with unlimited transfers. However, if you plan on using public transportation frequently, consider purchasing a Paris Visite pass, a Navigo card, or a carnet (a book of 10 single tickets) to save money. The Paris Visite pass provides unlimited travel on public transportation for a set number of days, and it also includes discounts on certain attractions.

Walking is another great way to see the city and save money. Paris is a very walkable city, and many of the major attractions are within a reasonable distance from one another.

Free Attractions

Paris is home to many world-famous attractions that are, unfortunately, quite expensive. However, there are also plenty of free attractions to enjoy in the city. Many of Paris's most famous landmarks, such as the Eiffel Tower, Notre-Dame Cathedral, and Sacré-Cœur Basilica, are free to admire from the outside. Additionally, several museums and attractions offer free admission on the first Sunday of every month, including the Louvre Museum and the Musée d'Orsay.

Paris is also home to many beautiful parks and gardens, such as the Luxembourg Gardens, Parc des Buttes-Chaumont, and Parc de la Villette, which are all free to enter and perfect for a leisurely stroll or a picnic.

Budget Shopping

Paris is a shopper's paradise, but it can also be quite expensive. However, there are several ways to shop on a budget. One of the best ways to save money is to shop at flea markets and thrift stores. Paris is home to several famous flea markets, such as the Marché aux Puces de Saint-Ouen and the Marché aux Puces de la Porte de Vanves, where you can find a wide variety of vintage and second-hand items at reasonable prices.

Another way to save money on shopping is to visit the many boutiques and independent shops in areas such as Le Marais and the Latin Quarter. These areas offer a wide variety of unique and affordable items that you won't find in the big department stores.

Also, don't forget to check out the sales! Sales in Paris are regulated by the government and only occur twice a year, in January and July. During these times, you can find great deals on clothing, accessories, and other items.

Cheap Flight and Train Tips

Travelling to Paris doesn't have to break the bank. With a bit of planning and flexibility, you can find affordable options for both flights and trains. Here are some tips to help you save on transportation:

- ▶ Be Flexible: Flexibility with your travel dates and times can lead to significant savings. Midweek flights and trains are usually cheaper than weekend ones. Also, consider travelling during off-peak hours.
- ▶ Book in Advance: Flight and train prices tend to increase as the travel date approaches. Try to book your tickets as early as possible to get the best deals.

- Compare Prices: Use online travel agencies and comparison websites to compare prices from different airlines and train operators. Sometimes it's cheaper to book a flight or train to a nearby city and then take a local train or bus to Paris.
- Consider Nearby Airports: Paris is served by two main airports, Charles de Gaulle (CDG) and Orly (ORY). Sometimes you can find cheaper flights to and from these airports. Also, consider airports in nearby cities like Brussels, Amsterdam, or London, and then take a train to Paris.
- Use Low-Cost Carriers: Consider using low-cost airlines for flights to and from Paris. Just be aware of the additional fees that low-cost carriers often charge.

Discount Cards

Paris offers several discount cards that can help you save money on attractions, transportation, and dining. Here are a few to consider:

- Paris Pass: This is a comprehensive sightseeing pass that includes free entry to over 60 attractions, a hop-on-hop-off bus tour, and unlimited travel on public transportation. It is available for 2, 3, 4, or 6 consecutive days.
- Paris Museum Pass: This pass provides free entry to over 50 museums and monuments in Paris and the surrounding region. It is available for 2, 4, or 6 consecutive days.
- Navigo Pass: This is a weekly or monthly transportation pass that provides unlimited travel on public transportation in Paris and the surrounding region.
- Paris Visite Pass: This is a travel card that provides unlimited travel on public transportation in Paris and the sur-

rounding region. It also includes discounts on certain attractions and is available for 1, 2, 3, or 5 consecutive days.

Off-Season Travel

Travelling to Paris during the off-season can lead to significant savings on accommodation, attractions, and dining. The peak tourist seasons in Paris are during the spring (April to June) and fall (September to November). Travelling during the winter months (December to February) or the summer months (July and August) can lead to lower prices and fewer crowds.

Just be prepared for the weather, as it can be quite cold in the winter and hot in the summer. Also, keep in mind that some attractions may have reduced hours or be closed during the off-season.

Final Thoughts

Visiting Paris on a budget may seem like a daunting task, given the city's reputation for being one of the most expensive in the world. However, with a little planning and some insider tips, it is entirely possible to enjoy the magic of Paris without breaking the bank. In this chapter, we've covered a range of budget-friendly options, from accommodation and dining to transportation and attractions. Remember to consider staying in budget accommodation, eating at more affordable establishments, using public transportation, visiting free attractions, and shopping at budget-friendly stores. Also, consider travelling during the off-season and taking advantage of various discount cards available.

Paris' charm lies not only in its luxurious boutiques and high-end restaurants but also in its charming streets, historic monuments, and the daily life of its inhabitants. Exploring the city on foot, picnicking in its beautiful parks, and taking in the street art are all free activities that can help you soak up the atmosphere of Paris without spending a cent. Additionally, many of the city's most famous attractions, such as the Notre Dame Cathedral, Sacré-Cœur Basilica, and the Champs-Elysées, are free to visit. Also, consider visiting the city's markets, where you can find fresh produce, local delicacies, and unique souvenirs at a fraction of the price of the touristy areas.

In conclusion, while Paris is undoubtedly a city that can be expensive, it is also a city that can be explored on a budget. With a bit of planning, some insider knowledge, and a willingness to explore off the beaten path, you can experience the best that Paris has to offer without emptying your wallet. Remember to plan ahead, be flexible, and take advantage of the many budget-friendly options available. After all, the beauty of Paris lies in its ability to enchant every visitor, regardless of their budget.

CHAPTER 12: 10 CULTURAL EXPERIENCES TO TRY

CHAPTER 12:
10 Cultural Experiences You Must Try in Paris

Paris is not only the capital of France but also a global hub for culture and the arts. The city has a rich history of fostering creativity and has been home to many of the world's most famous artists, writers, musicians, and filmmakers.

Today, Paris continues to be a vibrant center for cultural expression, offering a wide range of experiences for both locals and visitors alike. In this chapter, we will explore ten cultural experiences that you can enjoy while in Paris, from cinema and music to theatre, literature, and more. Each of these experiences will give you a deeper insight into the French culture and help you appreciate the city on a whole new level.

1 - French Cinema

French cinema has a long and storied history, dating back to the late 19th century when the Lumière brothers invented the cinematograph. Since then, France has been a pioneer in the world of cinema, producing many iconic films and filmmakers such as François Truffaut, Jean-Luc Godard, and Agnès Varda. While in Paris, consider visiting La Cinémathèque Française, a film museum and cinema that houses one of the largest collections of film documents and memorabilia in the world. You can also catch a movie at one of the city's historic cinemas, such as Le Grand Rex or Le Champo.

In addition to its rich history, French cinema continues to be vibrant and innovative today. Consider watching a contemporary French film at one of the many cinemas throughout the city or attending a film festival, such as the Paris Film Festival or the Festival du Film de Paris. Watching a French film, whether it be a classic or a contemporary work, is a great way to immerse yourself in the French language and culture.

2 - French Music

French music is as varied and diverse as the country itself, with a rich tradition of classical music, chanson française (French song), jazz, and electronic music. Paris has been home to many famous composers, such as Maurice Ravel, Claude Debussy, and Édith Piaf, and continues to be a center for musical innovation today. Consider attending a concert at one of the city's historic venues, such as the Opéra Garnier or the Philharmonie de Paris. In addition to classical music, Paris has a vibrant contemporary music scene. From jazz clubs in Saint-Germain-des-Prés to electronic music venues in the Marais, there is something for everyone. Consider checking out the lineup at popular venues such as Le Batofar, Le Rex Club, or La Bellevilloise. Also, don't forget to explore the city's many record shops, where you can discover new music and pick up a souvenir to remember your trip by.

Whether you are a fan of classical music, jazz, electronic, or anything in between, Paris has a wide range of musical experiences to offer. Attending a concert, exploring the city's music venues, or simply enjoying some music at a café are all great ways to immerse yourself in the French music culture.

3 - French Theatre

The French theatre has a rich and varied history that dates back to the Middle Ages. Over the centuries, it has evolved and adapted to changing tastes and societal norms, resulting in a diverse and dynamic theatre scene that is alive and well today. From classic plays by Molière and Racine to contemporary works by Yasmina Reza and Florian Zeller, French theatre offers something for everyone. Consider catching a play at one of the city's historic theatres, such as the Comédie-Française or the Théâtre de l'Odéon.

In addition to traditional theatre, Paris also has a vibrant scene for alternative and experimental theatre. Venues such as Théâtre de la Ville and Théâtre du Châtelet regularly host innovative productions that push the boundaries of what is possible on stage. If you are looking for something a bit different, consider attending a performance by a physical theatre or contemporary dance company.

Whether you are a fan of classic plays, contemporary works, or experimental productions, the Parisian theatre scene has something to offer. Attending a play or a performance is a great way to immerse yourself in the French language and culture while enjoying a night out on the town.

4 - French Literature

French literature has a long and illustrious history, with many famous writers hailing from the country, such as Victor Hugo,

Marcel Proust, and Simone de Beauvoir. Paris, in particular, has been a magnet for writers, both French and foreign, who have been inspired by the city's atmosphere and vibrant intellectual scene. Consider visiting the former homes and haunts of famous writers, such as the Maison de Victor Hugo or the Café de Flore.

In addition to its rich literary history, Paris continues to be a center for contemporary literature. The city is home to many bookstores, publishing houses, and literary events, such as the Paris Book Fair and the Festival Quartier du Livre. Consider picking up a book by a contemporary French author or attending a book signing or a reading.

Whether you are a fan of classic literature or contemporary works, Paris has a wide range of literary experiences to offer. Visiting the former homes of famous writers, exploring the city's bookstores, or attending a literary event are all great ways to immerse yourself in the French literary culture.

5 - Wine Tasting

French wine is renowned worldwide for its quality and variety. From the vineyards of Bordeaux to the Champagne region, France produces some of the best wines in the world. Paris, being the capital, offers a wide range of wine-tasting experiences, from traditional wine bars and cellars to more modern and innovative spaces. Consider visiting a historic wine cellar, such as Les Caves du Louvre, where you can learn about the wine-making process and taste a selection of wines.

In addition to traditional wine-tasting experiences, Paris also offers more innovative options. For example, consider attending a wine-tasting workshop, where you can learn about the different grape varieties, regions, and tasting techniques. Alternatively, you can also book a wine-tasting tour, which will take you to different wine bars and cellars throughout the city.

Whether you are a wine connoisseur or a casual enthusiast, Paris offers a wide range of wine-tasting experiences to suit all tastes and budgets. Attending a wine-tasting workshop, visiting a historic wine cellar, or exploring the city's wine bars are all great ways to immerse yourself in the French wine culture.

6 - Fashion Shows

Paris is synonymous with fashion, and it has been the epicenter of the fashion world for centuries. The city is home to some of the most famous fashion houses in the world, such as Chanel, Louis Vuitton, and Dior. Twice a year, Paris hosts Fashion Week, a major event that attracts designers, models, and fashion enthusiasts from all over the world. If you are lucky enough to be in Paris during Fashion Week, consider attending a fashion show or an after-party.

In addition to Fashion Week, Paris also has a number of boutiques, showrooms, and concept stores that showcase the work of emerging designers. Consider visiting Leclaireur or Merci, where you can discover unique pieces and get a sense of the latest trends. Also, don't forget to visit the Palais Galliera, the city's fashion museum, which regularly hosts exhibitions on various aspects of fashion history and design.

Whether you are a fashion aficionado or simply interested in discovering the latest trends, Paris offers a wide range of fashion-related experiences.

7 - French Language

The French language is an essential part of French culture and identity. It is the official language of France and is spoken by about 220 million people worldwide. If you are visiting Paris and want to improve your French, consider taking a language course at one of the city's language schools, such as Alliance Française or L'École Internationale de Paris.

In addition to formal language courses, there are also many informal ways to practice your French in Paris. Consider joining a language exchange group, attending a language café, or simply striking up a conversation with a local. Also, don't forget to take advantage of the many cultural experiences that Paris has to offer, such as attending a play, a concert, or a film screening, all of which can help improve your language skills.

Whether you are a beginner or an advanced speaker, Paris offers a wide range of opportunities to improve your French language skills. Taking a language course, attending a language exchange event, or simply practicing your French in everyday situations are all great ways to enjoy your trip.

8 - French Sports

Sports play an important role in French culture, and Paris is home to some of the most famous sports teams and venues in the world. Football is the most popular sport in France, and Paris is home to Paris Saint-Germain (PSG), one of the most successful football clubs in Europe. Consider attending a football match at the Parc des Princes, the home stadium of PSG.

In addition to football, Paris also has a vibrant rugby scene. The city is home to two major rugby clubs, Stade Français and

Racing 92. If you are a rugby fan, consider attending a match at the Stade Jean-Bouin or the Paris La Défense Arena. Additionally, Paris hosts the final stage of the Tour de France, the world's most famous cycling race, every year in July. Watching the final stage on the Champs-Élysées is a must-do experience for any cycling enthusiast.

Whether you are a football, rugby, or cycling enthusiast, Paris offers a wide range of sporting experiences. Attending a match, a race, or a sporting event is a great way to enjoy a bit of friendly competition.

9 - French Festivals

France is known for its diverse range of festivals, many of which are held in Paris. From music and film to food and wine, there is a festival for everyone in the French capital. One of the most famous is the Fête de la Musique, a nationwide music festival held on the first day of summer. Musicians of all genres take to the streets, squares, and parks of Paris to perform free concerts, making it a great opportunity to discover new artists and enjoy music in a festive atmosphere.

Another major event is the Nuit Blanche, an annual all-night arts festival held in October. Museums, galleries, and public spaces across the city stay open all night, hosting exhibitions, performances, and installations. It's a unique opportunity to explore Paris by night and see the city in a new light. Additionally, the Bastille Day celebrations on July 14th, which include a military parade on the Champs-Élysées and fireworks at the Eiffel Tower, are not to be missed.

Whether you are a music lover, an art enthusiast, or a foodie, Paris has a festival for you. Attending a festival is a great way to immerse yourself in French culture, meet locals, and have a memorable experience in the City of Light.

10 - French Architecture

Paris is a city with a rich architectural heritage, from medieval buildings to modern skyscrapers. The city is home to some of the most iconic landmarks in the world, such as the Eiffel Tower, Notre-Dame Cathedral, and the Sacré-Cœur Basilica. Consider taking a guided tour or a river cruise to learn more about the history and architecture of these iconic buildings.

In addition to its famous landmarks, Paris is also home to many lesser-known architectural gems. Consider visiting the Fondation Louis Vuitton, a contemporary art museum designed by Frank Gehry, or the Musée d'Orsay, a former railway station turned art museum. Also, don't forget to explore the different neighborhoods of Paris, each with its own architectural style and character. From the Haussmannian buildings of the Right Bank to the modernist architecture of La Défense, Paris offers a wide range of architectural experiences.

Whether you are an architecture enthusiast or simply interested in discovering the history of Paris, the city offers a wide range of architectural experiences. Taking a guided tour, visiting a museum, or simply exploring the city on foot are all great ways to immerse yourself in the architecture of Paris.

CHAPTER 13:
Parisian Walks

. . . .

Paris, the City of Lights, is a city best discovered on foot. The intricate layout of its neighborhoods, the narrow cobblestone streets, and the stunning architecture that surrounds you at every turn make walking one of the best ways to explore Paris. This chapter aims to guide you through different neighborhoods in Paris, detailing routes that pass by various attractions, cafes, and boutiques. Each walk is designed to provide a unique perspective of the city, from the historic and artistic Montmartre to the hipster vibes of Canal St-Martin. So, lace up your walking shoes, grab a map, and let's embark on an adventure through the streets of Paris!

Tips for Walking in Paris

Before you set out on your Parisian adventure, here are some tips to make your walks more enjoyable and comfortable:

1. Wear Comfortable Shoes: Parisian streets are often cobblestoned and can be tough on your feet. Make sure to wear comfortable, sturdy shoes to make your walk more enjoyable.
2. Stay Hydrated: Walking can be tiring, especially during the summer months. Carry a bottle of water with you to stay hydrated.

3. Take Breaks: Don't rush! Take your time and enjoy the scenery. Stop at a café, rest your feet, and soak in the atmosphere.

4. Use a Map: While getting lost in Paris can be a delightful adventure, having a map or a navigation app on your phone can be helpful to find your way and ensure you don't miss any points of interest.

5. Be Aware of Your Surroundings: Keep an eye on your belongings and be aware of your surroundings. Paris is generally a safe city, but like any other major city, it has its share of pickpockets.

6. Respect the Locals: Remember that Paris is a bustling city with people going about their daily lives. Be mindful not to block the sidewalks or doorways, and try to keep noise levels down.

Remember, the journey is as important as the destination. Take your time, enjoy the walk, and discover the hidden gems of Paris!

1 - Montmartre Walk

The Montmartre neighborhood is famous for its bohemian atmosphere, historic sites, and stunning views of Paris. This walk will take you through the most iconic spots in Montmartre and provide a glimpse into the artistic and historic heart of Paris.

- ▶ Duration: 2-3 hours
- ▶ Difficulty: Moderate (Some steep hills)
- ▶ Start: Abbesses Metro Station
- ▶ End: Lamarck-Caulaincourt Metro Station

Route

Start at Abbesses Metro Station and head to the Place des Abbesses to visit the Wall of "I Love Yous".
From there, walk to the Place du Tertre, a square famous for its artists and portraitists.
Continue to the Sacré-Cœur Basilica, where you can enjoy a panoramic view of Paris.
Descend the hill to visit the Montmartre Vineyards.
Walk past the former homes of famous artists like Picasso and Van Gogh on Rue Lepic.
End your walk at the Lamarck-Caulaincourt Metro Station.

Points of Interest

- ▶ Wall of "I Love Yous"
- ▶ Place du Tertre
- ▶ Sacré-Cœur Basilica
- ▶ Montmartre Vineyards
- ▶ Former homes of Picasso and Van Gogh on Rue Lepic

2 - Le Marais Stroll

Le Marais is one of the oldest and most beautiful neighborhoods in Paris. This walk will take you through its narrow medieval streets, past historic mansions, trendy boutiques, and lively squares.

- ▶ Duration: 2 hours
- ▶ Difficulty: Easy
- ▶ Start: Hôtel de Ville Metro Station
- ▶ End: Saint-Paul Metro Station

. . . .

Route

Start at the Hôtel de Ville Metro Station and walk to the Hôtel de Ville (City Hall).
Continue to the Place des Vosges, the oldest planned square in Paris.
Visit the Maison de Victor Hugo, where the famous author once lived.
Walk down Rue des Rosiers, the heart of the Jewish quarter.
Continue to the Place de la Bastille and the July Column.
End your walk at the Saint-Paul Metro Station.

Points of Interest

- ▶ Hôtel de Ville (City Hall)
- ▶ Place des Vosges
- ▶ Maison de Victor Hugo
- ▶ Rue des Rosiers
- ▶ Place de la Bastille and July Column

. . . .

3 - Latin Quarter Wander

The Latin Quarter is the historic student quarter of Paris, home to the Sorbonne University and many other educational institutions. This walk will take you past historic sites, lively squares, and charming bookshops.

- ▶ Duration: 2 hours
- ▶ Difficulty: Easy
- ▶ Start: Saint-Michel Metro Station
- ▶ End: Jussieu Metro Station

. . . .

Route

Start at the Saint-Michel Metro Station and visit the Fontaine Saint-Michel.

Walk to the Place Saint-Michel and then continue to the Luxembourg Gardens.

Visit the Panthéon, the final resting place of many famous French citizens.

Walk down Rue Mouffetard, a lively street with many shops and cafes.

End your walk at the Jussieu Metro Station.

Points of Interest

- ▶ Fontaine Saint-Michel
- ▶ Place Saint-Michel
- ▶ Luxembourg Gardens
- ▶ Panthéon
- ▶ Rue Mouffetard

. . . .

4 - St-Germain-des-Prés Promenade

St-Germain-des-Prés is known for its literary history, chic boutiques, and charming cafes. This walk will take you through its most iconic spots, past famous landmarks, and into its hidden courtyards.

- ▶ Duration: 2 hours
- ▶ Difficulty: Easy
- ▶ Start: Saint-Germain-des-Prés Metro Station
- ▶ End: Mabillon Metro Station

. . . .

Route

Start at the Saint-Germain-des-Prés Metro Station and visit the Church of Saint-Germain-des-Prés.
Walk to the Les Deux Magots and Café de Flore, two famous cafes frequented by intellectuals and artists in the past.
Continue to the Luxembourg Gardens, a beautiful park perfect for a leisurely stroll.
Walk down Rue de Seine, known for its art galleries and antique shops.
End your walk at the Mabillon Metro Station.

Points of Interest

- ▶ Church of Saint-Germain-des-Prés
- ▶ Les Deux Magots and Café de Flore
- ▶ Luxembourg Gardens
- ▶ Rue de Seine

. . . .

5 - Canal St-Martin Amble

The Canal St-Martin area is known for its picturesque canals, trendy boutiques, and lively cafes. This walk will take you along the canal, past historic sites, and into some of the neighborhood's most vibrant areas.

- ▶ Duration: 2 hours
- ▶ Difficulty: Easy
- ▶ Start: République Metro Station
- ▶ End: Jaurès Metro Station

· ·

Route

Start at the République Metro Station and walk to the Place de la République.
Continue to the Canal St-Martin and walk along its banks.
Visit the Hôpital Saint-Louis, one of the oldest hospitals in Paris.
Continue to the Parc de la Villette, home to the Cité des Sciences et de l'Industrie and the Philharmonie de Paris.
End your walk at the Jaurès Metro Station.

Points of Interest

- ▶ Place de la République
- ▶ Canal St-Martin
- ▶ Hôpital Saint-Louis
- ▶ Parc de la Villette

· ·

6 - Belleville Ramble

Belleville is a diverse and vibrant neighborhood known for its street art, lively atmosphere, and stunning views of Paris. This walk will take you through its most iconic spots, past famous landmarks, and into its hidden corners.

- Duration: 2-3 hours
- Difficulty: Moderate (Some steep hills)
- Start: Belleville Metro Station
- End: Pyrénées Metro Station

. . . .

Route

Start at the Belleville Metro Station and visit the Parc de Belleville, which offers a panoramic view of Paris.
Walk down Rue Denoyez, known for its street art and artist workshops.
Continue to the Edith Piaf Museum, dedicated to the famous French singer.
Visit the Belleville Market, a lively outdoor market.
End your walk at the Pyrénées Metro Station.

Points of Interest

- Parc de Belleville
- Rue Denoyez
- Edith Piaf Museum
- Belleville Market

. . . .

7 - Île de la Cité and Île Saint-Louis Saunter

These two islands in the Seine are the historical heart of Paris, home to some of its most iconic landmarks. This leisurely walk will take you through charming streets, past stunning architecture, and along the scenic riverbanks.

- ▶ Duration: 1.5-2 hours
- ▶ Difficulty: Easy
- ▶ Start: Cité Metro Station
- ▶ End: Pont Marie Metro Station

. . . .

Route

Start at the Cité Metro Station and visit the Notre-Dame Cathedral.
Walk to the Palais de Justice and the Sainte-Chapelle.
Continue to the Place Dauphine, a tranquil square.
Cross the Pont Saint-Louis to Île Saint-Louis.
Explore the main street, Rue Saint-Louis en l'Île, known for its boutiques, galleries, and cafes.
End your walk at the Pont Marie Metro Station.

Points of Interest

- ▶ Notre-Dame Cathedral
- ▶ Palais de Justice and Sainte-Chapelle
- ▶ Place Dauphine
- ▶ Rue Saint-Louis en l'Île

. . . .

8 - Champs-Élysées and Tuileries Trek

This walk takes you along one of the world's most famous avenue, past luxurious shops and historic monuments, and through a beautiful garden.

- ▶ Duration: 2-3 hours
- ▶ Difficulty: Easy
- ▶ Start: Arc de Triomphe
- ▶ End: Musée du Louvre

. . . .

Route

Start at the Arc de Triomphe and walk down the Champs-Élysées.
Visit the Grand Palais and the Petit Palais.
Continue to the Place de la Concorde, where you can see the Obelisk of Luxor.
Walk through the Tuileries Garden, past sculptures, fountains, and ponds.
End your walk at the Musée du Louvre.

Points of Interest

- ▶ Arc de Triomphe
- ▶ Grand Palais and Petit Palais
- ▶ Place de la Concorde
- ▶ Tuileries Garden
- ▶ Musée du Louvre

. . . .

Final Thoughts

Walking is undoubtedly one of the best ways to explore Paris. Each neighborhood has its own distinct charm and character, and walking allows you to experience the city on a more intimate level. The itineraries detailed in this chapter are just a starting point – there are countless other routes to discover and explore. Don't be afraid to wander off the beaten path and get lost in the streets of Paris. You never know what hidden gem you might stumble upon.

While walking, you'll get to see the evolution of Parisian architecture, from the medieval structures on the Île de la Cité to the grand Haussmannian buildings that line the Champs-Élysées. You'll pass by iconic landmarks, bustling local markets, and quiet residential streets. You'll encounter the hustle and bustle of daily life, as well as the calm and serenity of the city's parks and gardens.

Remember to take breaks when needed, stay hydrated, and always have a map or navigation app on hand. Also, consider the weather and dress accordingly. Paris can be quite hot in the summer and very cold in the winter, so plan your walks accordingly.

Walking through Paris is not just a way to see the sights, but also a way to feel the rhythm of the city, to soak up its atmosphere, and to truly understand what makes it so special. From the romantic streets of Montmartre to the trendy boutiques in Le Marais, the intellectual history of the Latin Quarter to the artistic vibe of St-Germain-des-Prés, each walk will offer a different perspective of Paris.

And as you walk, don't forget to look up. Paris is a city of details, from the intricate ironwork on the balconies to the sculptures that adorn the facades of buildings. Take the time to appreciate these details, as they are part of what makes Paris so unique.

In conclusion, Paris is a city that is meant to be explored on foot. Whether you are visiting for the first time or have been many times before, there is always something new to discover. We hope that this chapter has inspired you to lace up your walking shoes and hit the streets of Paris. Bon voyage!

CHAPTER 14:
Recommended Itinerary in Paris

Planning a trip to Paris can be both exciting and overwhelming. With so many iconic landmarks, world-class museums, and charming neighborhoods to explore, it can be hard to know where to start. This recommended itinerary is designed to help you make the most of your time in the City of Light, whether you are visiting for a weekend or an entire week. It includes a mix of must-see attractions, local favorites, and hidden gems, as well as tips on where to eat and how to get around.

Before you start planning your itinerary, there are a few things to consider. First, decide how many days you have in Paris. This will help you determine how much you can realistically see and do. Next, think about your priorities. Are you interested in art and history, or are you more of a food and shopping person? Do you want to see the main tourist attractions or do you prefer to explore off the beaten path? Once you have a clear idea of your interests and priorities, you can start planning your itinerary.

3-Day Itinerary

Day 1

▸ **Morning**: Eiffel Tower and Trocadéro
Start your day by visiting the most iconic landmark in Paris, the Eiffel Tower. Arrive early to avoid the crowds and take the elevator or the stairs to the top for panoramic views of the city. Afterwards, head to the Trocadéro Gardens, located just across the Seine River from the Eiffel Tower. This is one of the best spots in Paris for taking photos of the tower.

▸ **Afternoon**: Seine River Cruise and Notre-Dame Cathedral
In the afternoon, take a Seine River cruise to see some of the most famous landmarks of Paris from the water. Many companies offer 1-hour cruises starting from the Eiffel Tower or Notre-Dame Cathedral. After the cruise, visit the Notre-Dame Cathedral on Île de la Cité. Although the cathedral was damaged by a fire in 2019, its façade and towers are still accessible to visitors.

▸ **Evening**: Latin Quarter and Dinner at a Traditional Bistro
In the evening, explore the Latin Quarter, one of the oldest and most charming neighborhoods in Paris. Wander through its narrow streets, visit its historic sites, such as the Pantheon, and enjoy dinner at a traditional French bistro.

Day 2

▶ **Morning**: Louvre Museum
Start your second day in Paris with a visit to the Louvre Museum, the world's largest and most visited art museum. It is home to thousands of works of art, including the Mona Lisa and the Venus de Milo. To make the most of your visit, consider booking a guided tour or doing some research in advance to decide which artworks and galleries you want to see.

▶ **Afternoon**: Le Marais and Picasso Museum
In the afternoon, head to Le Marais, one of the most fashionable and historic neighborhoods in Paris. Explore its boutiques, art galleries, and historic mansions, and visit the Picasso Museum, which houses one of the largest collections of Picasso's artworks in the world.

▶ **Evening**: Montmartre and Sacré-Cœur Basilica
In the evening, head to Montmartre, a historic and bohemian neighborhood located on a hill in the north of Paris. Visit the Sacré-Cœur Basilica, enjoy the views of the city from its steps, and explore the neighborhood's artists' studios, cafes, and cabarets.

Day 3

▶ **Morning**: Champs-Élysées and Arc de Triomphe
Start your third day in Paris with a walk down the Champs-Élysées, one of the most famous avenues in the world. Visit the Arc de Triomphe, located at the western end of the avenue, and climb to the top for panoramic views of Paris.

▸ **Afternoon**: Orsay Museum and Tuileries Garden

In the afternoon, visit the Orsay Museum, located in a former railway station on the left bank of the Seine River. It houses an extensive collection of Impressionist and Post-Impressionist masterpieces by artists such as Monet, Van Gogh, and Degas. After your visit, take a walk in the Tuileries Garden, located between the Louvre Museum and the Place de la Concorde.

▸ **Evening**: Opera Garnier and Galeries Lafayette

In the evening, visit the Opera Garnier, one of the most beautiful buildings in Paris, and take a guided tour of its opulent interior. Afterwards, head to the Galeries Lafayette, a famous department store located nearby. Visit its rooftop terrace for panoramic views of the city and do some shopping.

5-Day Itinerary

Day 4

▸ **Morning**: Day Trip to Versailles
On the fourth day, take a day trip to the Palace of Versailles, located about 20 kilometers southwest of Paris. The palace is one of the most famous and opulent royal residences in the world and a UNESCO World Heritage site. Explore the palace, its stunning Hall of Mirrors, and its beautiful gardens. If you have time, visit the Grand Trianon and the Petit Trianon, two smaller palaces located on the grounds of Versailles.

▸ **Afternoon**: Shopping in Le Marais
In the afternoon, head back to Paris and do some shopping in Le Marais. This neighborhood is known for its trendy boutiques, art galleries, and vintage shops. It's a great place to find unique souvenirs, fashion, and home decor.

▸ **Evening**: Dinner at a Gourmet Restaurant
In the evening, treat yourself to dinner at a gourmet restaurant. Paris is home to many Michelin-starred restaurants, but there are also plenty of other excellent dining options to choose from. Be sure to make a reservation in advance.

Day 5

▸ **Morning**: Pantheon and Luxembourg Gardens
Start your last day in Paris with a visit to the Pantheon, a historic mausoleum located in the Latin Quarter. It is the final resting

place of many famous French figures, such as Voltaire, Rousseau, and Zola. Afterwards, take a walk in the Luxembourg Gardens, one of the most beautiful parks in Paris.

- ▸ **Afternoon**: Sainte-Chapelle and Île de la Cité

In the afternoon, visit the Sainte-Chapelle, a Gothic chapel located on the Île de la Cité. It is famous for its stunning stained glass windows. Afterwards, explore the Île de la Cité, the historic heart of Paris. Visit the Conciergerie, a former royal palace and prison, and take a walk along the Seine River.

- ▸ **Evening**: Seine River Banks and Pont Alexandre III

In the evening, take a leisurely stroll along the banks of the Seine River. This is one of the most romantic activities to do in Paris, especially at sunset. Walk across the Pont Alexandre III, one of the most beautiful bridges in Paris, and enjoy the views of the Eiffel Tower and the Grand Palais.

Final Thoughts

As your time in Paris comes to an end, you might find yourself feeling a mix of emotions. Joy, for all the unforgettable experiences you've had, and perhaps a touch of sadness, that your adventure in one of the world's most beautiful cities is drawing to a close. Paris has a way of capturing your heart and it's not uncommon to feel a longing to stay just a little bit longer.

Whether you spent your time marveling at world-renowned landmarks, exploring art galleries, savoring delicious French cuisine, or simply wandering through its charming streets, Paris undoubtedly left a lasting impression on you. It's a city of history, culture, romance, and so much more. Every corner you turned, every pastry you tasted, every cobblestone street you walked down, contributed to your unique Parisian adventure.

We hope that this itinerary served as a helpful guide, but also that it encouraged you to explore on your own terms, and maybe even discover some hidden gems along the way. Paris is a city that always has something new to offer, and each visit can be a different experience. There are always more neighborhoods to explore, more restaurants to try, more pieces of art to admire, and more beautiful views to take in.

Perhaps you discovered a love for French cinema, a new favorite wine, or an appreciation for Impressionist art. Maybe you found inspiration in the city's architecture, felt a connection to its history, or simply enjoyed the relaxed pace of life in a Parisian café. Whatever your experience, it was uniquely yours, and that's what makes Paris so special.

Remember to leave a little piece of your heart in Paris, as a promise to yourself that you'll return one day. And when you do, Paris will be there, ready to unveil new secrets, share more of its magic, and offer new memories to be made.

As you board your plane or train and say au revoir to Paris, reflect on your adventure and start dreaming of your next one. After all, travel is not just about the destinations we visit, but about the person we become along the way. Bon voyage!

Conclusion

As we conclude this guide, we reflect on the rich and diverse tapestry that is Paris, a city that embodies the essence of culture, romance, art, and gastronomy. Each neighborhood, each monument, each café, has its own unique charm and story to tell. Yet, it is the collective spirit of Paris, that undeniable 'je ne sais quoi,' that leaves a lasting impression on every visitor. Paris is more than just a destination; it is an experience, a journey through history, a feast for the senses, and a celebration of life.

Remember, travel is not just about ticking off a list of attractions or activities. It's about immersing yourself in the local culture, interacting with the people, and opening your heart and mind to new experiences and perspectives. Paris offers a plethora of opportunities for such meaningful engagements, whether it's savoring a buttery croissant in a neighborhood boulangerie, admiring the intricate details of Gothic architecture, or strolling along the Seine River at sunset.

In Paris, every season has its charm, and there's always something happening, from the lively Fête de la Musique in June to the elegant Nuit Blanche in October, and the festive Christmas markets in December. These events offer a unique opportunity to dive deep into Parisian traditions and customs, far beyond the typical tourist path.

Exploring Paris doesn't have to break the bank. Embrace the Parisian way of life to save money and enhance your experience. This could mean opting for a 'formule' at lunch, taking advantage of the free first Sundays at many museums, shopping at local markets, or using public transport to get around. Don't hesitate to venture off the beaten path - some of the most rewarding experiences often lie away from the main tourist routes.

As for the language, don't worry if you don't speak fluent French. While learning a few basic phrases can go a long way in creating a connection with the locals, Parisians are generally understanding, even when faced with a language barrier. And who knows? You might find yourself picking up more French than you expected by the end of your trip.

To help you along the way, here are some basic phrases that can be useful for any traveler in Paris:

- Où est...? (Where is...?)

- Combien ça coûte? (How much does it cost?)

- Parlez-vous anglais? (Do you speak English?)

- Pouvez-vous m'aider? (Can you help me?)

- Je ne comprends pas. (I don't understand.)

- Je suis perdu(e). (I'm lost.)

- Où sont les toilettes? (Where are the toilets?)

- Puis-je voir la carte, s'il vous plaît? (Can I see the menu, please?)

- Je voudrais... (I would like...)

- Merci. (Thank you.)

- ▷ De rien. (You're welcome.)

- ▷ S'il vous plaît. (Please.)

- ▷ Excusez-moi. (Excuse me.)

- ▷ Comment ça s'appelle? (What is this called?)

- ▷ Comment aller à...? (How do I get to...?)

Remember, it's the effort and the intention to communicate that often matters more than perfect grammar or pronunciation. So don't be afraid to try out your French - it's all part of the adventure!

The culinary scene in Paris is a delight for both gourmands and casual food lovers. From the bustling food markets to the cozy bistros and the world-renowned restaurants, the gastronomic offerings of Paris are endless. Remember that meal times in Paris are usually later than in many other countries, so adapt to the local rhythm to truly savor the culinary delights that Paris has to offer.

Art and culture in Paris are not confined to museums or galleries; they are everywhere, in the grand boulevards, the hidden courtyards, the music that fills the air, and the way Parisians enjoy their leisure time. The cultural wealth of Paris is indeed astounding, and no matter how much time you spend here, there will always be something new to discover, to admire, to fall in love with.

Lastly, take your time and savor every moment. Paris is not a place to be rushed. It's a place to linger over a leisurely lunch, to relax in a beautiful garden, to stroll along the riverbank as the sun sets, to dance the night away under a sky full of stars. It's a place to live in the moment, to feel the pulse of life, to breathe in the air of history and tradition, and to let the Parisian spirit seep into your soul.

With its rich cultural heritage, breathtaking landscapes, world-class art and music, vibrant neighborhoods, and gastronomic delights, Paris promises an unforgettable travel experience. But remember, Paris is not just a place to visit; it's a place to experience, to savor, and to love. So pack your bags, bring an open heart, and embark on the Parisian adventure that awaits you. And as you set foot on Parisian soil, remember the words of the famous French writer Victor Hugo: "Respirer Paris, cela conserve l'âme" - To breathe Paris preserves the soul.

Here's to a journey of a lifetime in Paris, a journey that will linger in your heart and soul long after you've returned home.

Final notes

You have reached the end of your journey through Paris, probably one of the most appreciated destinations among travelers from all over the world. We hope that the suggested destinations and our advice will help you plan and enjoy your trip through Paris to the fullest.

The travel guide series of the Journey Joy collection was designed to be lean and straight to the point. The idea of keeping the guides short required significant work in synthesis, in order to guide the reader towards the essential destinations and activities within each country and city.

If you liked the book, leaving a positive review can help us spread our work. We realize that leaving a review can be a tedious activity, so we want to give you a gift. Send an email to **bonus@dedaloagency.net**, attach the screenshot of your review, and you will get completely **FREE**, in your mailbox, **THE UNRELEASED EBOOK**: "The Art of Traveling: Essential Tips for Unforgettable Journeys".

Remember to check the Spam folder, as the email might end up there!

We thank you in advance and wish you to always travel and enjoy every adventure!

Made in United States
Orlando, FL
27 January 2024

42969775R00107